D1146978

AT HOME IN LENT

WINCHESTER SCHOOL OF MISSION

05533

The Bible Reading Fellowship
15 The Chambers, Vineyard
Abingdon OX14 3FE
brf.org.uk

The Bible Reading Fellowship (BRF) is a Registered Charity (233280)

ISBN 978 0 85746 589 4
First published 2018
10 9 8 7 6 5 4 3 2 1 0
All rights reserved

Text © Gordon Giles 2018
This edition © The Bible Reading Fellowship 2018
Cover image by Rebecca J Hall

The author asserts the moral right to be identified as the author of this work

Acknowledgements
Unless otherwise stated, scripture quotations are taken from The New Revised
Standard Version of the Bible, Anglicised edition, copyright © 1989, 1995 by the
Division of Christian Education of the National Council of the Churches of Christ in
the United States of America. Used by permission. All rights reserved.

Every effort has been made to trace and contact copyright owners for material used
in this resource. We apologise for any inadvertent omissions or errors, and would
ask those concerned to contact us so that full acknowledgement can be made in
the future.

A catalogue record for this book is available from the British Library

Printed and bound by CPI Group (UK) Ltd, Croydon CR0 4YY

AT HOME IN LENT

**An exploration of Lent
through 46 objects**

Gordon Giles

Contents

WEEK THREE

WEEK FOUR

WEEK FIVE

HOLY WEEK

EPILOGUE

Introduction

Is your home your spiritual castle? The origins of the proverb 'An Englishman's home is his castle' date back to the 16th century, when in 1581 Henri Estienne's *The Stage of Popish Toyes: conteining both tragicall and comicall partes*, stated that 'youre house is youre Castell', and in the same year Richard Mulcaster, the headmaster of the Merchant Taylor's School in London, wrote, 'He [the householder] is the appointer of his owne circumstance, and his house is his castle.' Seventy years later, the lawyer and politician Sir Edward Coke established the idea in law in *The Institutes of the Laws of England* (1628): 'For a man's house is his castle, *et domus sua cuique est tutissimum refugium* [and one's home is one's safest refuge].' Another century later and none other than William Pitt the Elder said in Parliament, 'The poorest man may in his cottage bid defiance to all the forces of the crown. It may be frail – its roof may shake – the wind may blow through it – the storm may enter – the rain may enter – but the King of England cannot enter.' The concept has carried across the seas to other lands too, notably to the USA, where in 1800 Joel Chandler Harris adapted the maxim, writing, 'Exalt the citizen. As the State is the unit of government, he is the unit of the State. Teach him that his home is his castle, and his sovereignty rests beneath his hat.'

Notwithstanding the modern right of the police and bailiffs to force their way into premises with the necessary warrant or court order, we generally believe and behave as though our homes are private and open only to those whom we invite in. In our homes, we flee from the presence of all but our nearest and dearest. While for some it can be a place of domestic violence, treachery or strife, for many the home is a sanctuary, a safe haven and the place where not only our hearts but also our belongings are housed. Increasingly, we have more and more possessions, and our homes are becoming warehouses for objects whose use, meaning and significance varies widely. It is said that nature abhors a vacuum; in modern times this means that no matter how big your home is, it will likely be full of stuff!

This book seeks to cross the threshold of the Christian home. By all means read it on the train, but its desire is to be invited in and its purpose is to snoop around and ask nosy questions about the things you have in your home. If we feel that our homes are our castles, open only to those we wish to invite in, then this book stands at the door knocking as a friend, a divine friend, even. For, as the psalmist reminds us, there is no place where we can flee from the presence of God:

> O Lord, you have searched me and known me.
> You know when I sit down and when I rise up;
>   you discern my thoughts from far away.
> You search out my path and my lying down,
>   and are acquainted with all my ways.
> Even before a word is on my tongue,
>   O Lord, you know it completely.
> You hem me in, behind and before,
>   and lay your hand upon me.
> Such knowledge is too wonderful for me;
>   it is so high that I cannot attain it.
>
> Where can I go from your spirit?
>   Or where can I flee from your presence?
> If I ascend to heaven, you are there;
>   if I make my bed in Sheol, you are there.
> If I take the wings of the morning
>   and settle at the farthest limits of the sea,
> even there your hand shall lead me,
>   and your right hand shall hold me fast.
> If I say, 'Surely the darkness shall cover me,
>   and the light around me become night,'
> even the darkness is not dark to you;

the night is as bright as the day,
for darkness is as light to you.

PSALM 139:1–12

Against the temptation to hide or flee from the Lord, this book of daily readings comes as an invitation to discover how he is already in our homes and as a map of where to seek and find God in the fixtures, fittings and other items with which we surround ourselves at home. Inspired by Neil MacGregor's 2010 BBC Radio 4 series *The History of the World in 100 Objects*, this book seeks to open access to the spiritual significance of 46 objects that can be found in almost any home. Our biblical ancestors did not have anything like as much 'stuff' as we do, but some of the things we possess have long histories, while other modern gadgets and household paraphernalia have something to say to us about the world in which we live and move and have our being, and about the God from whom all art and science comes. For the way we live is a spiritual as well as a practical matter, and under God it is good to reflect on the things we take so much for granted.

The Holy Spirit of God is everywhere and in everything, if we only look with the right eyes and a humble frame of mind. During Lent, we are called to read and reflect, to be penitent and patient, and to journey towards the renewing light of the Easter dawn. When Easter comes in seven weeks, it is my hope and prayer for you, gentle reader, that the journey around your home will cast Passiontide and Easter in a different hue, and that the Lord will have been with you in everything, and everywhere.

Ash Wednesday

Door

Behold, I stand and knock

'Listen! I am standing at the door, knocking; if you hear my voice and open the door, I will come in to you and eat with you, and you with me. To the one who conquers I will give a place with me on my throne, just as I myself conquered and sat down with my Father on his throne. Let anyone who has an ear listen to what the Spirit is saying to the churches.'
REVELATION 3:20–22

Have you ever paid any attention to your front door? The lock on mine broke recently, and then I suddenly became very interested in how it works, whether it would work and whether I would actually end up locked in or locked out. The little button on the catch broke off, and I lost confidence in the security, safety and convenience of a door that is opened and closed at least a dozen times a day. So I went to a locksmith and bought a new door lock, and then had some adventures getting the old one off and replacing it. All the while I was aware that if I were to make a mistake then the security of my family and possessions could be jeopardised. However holy-minded or spiritually aloof one tries to be about one's stuff, in the end we do worry about these things and in a modern society do need to be wary of risk and realistic about personal safety and valuables.

A front door is not just for keeping people out, of course; it is also for letting them in! As a parish vicar, I frequently open my door to people and have more visitors than most. Occasionally I have visitors who I don't want to, or should not, let in. I learnt the hard way to be at least a little wary. A stranger at the door invited himself in, and it turned out he was a violent criminal who wanted money. I had to give him some to make him leave, but I suppose he may have needed it. We all get unwelcome visitors from time to time, selling, buying, conning or manipulating, and we have to engage in that ongoing inner dialogue: 'Are they genuine? What is the real cost of mistakenly giving them something as opposed to shutting the door on real need?' It is better to be conned a bit than to contribute to someone's ongoing suffering.

When we read the words of Christ as heard by John in this passage from Revelation, they conjure up images of Jesus on our doorstep, knocking on a door that we have locked from the inside and only we can open. He does not batter the door or break it down. We may wonder whether he comes as stranger or friend. The artist William Holman Hunt (1827–1910), who lies buried in St Paul's Cathedral, painted many religious works, but the most famous is undoubtedly *The Light of the World*, of which there are several versions of various sizes. The largest one, which went on a world tour because it was so popular, now stands in the Middlesex Chapel of St Paul's, where it forms a backdrop to daily prayer. Sadly, it is poorly lit and not easy to attend to in detail, but the figure of Christ holding a lantern and knocking on a wooden door is clear enough. Momentary study reveals that the door has no handle: it can only be opened from within. The door is the door to our hearts, and knock as loudly as he might, only we can open the door and let Christ in.

It may be a sentimental picture, beloved of the Victorians and easy to feel warm inside about, but the metaphor can be pushed a little when we think of the front doors of our own homes. Generally, our doors are not merely closed; they are locked. Thus, to open them is a two-stage process. That also assumes that our door has oiled hinges, is unobstructed and that the lock works; that is, as well as our wanting to open the door, it must be physically possible to do so. For, like my vicarage door with the broken lock, our spiritual doors must be maintained and cared for. Generally, we don't pay attention to things until they break, but maintenance is vital. This, in a deep sense, is what this season of Lent is all about.

As we enter Lent, a period of penitence, self-reflection and self-denial, we may also like to think of it as a time for spiritual maintenance. It can be a seven-week period for making sure that we truly are 'at home' to Jesus, that the door of our hearts is open and that the rest of our spiritual home is in good working order. The word 'Lent' derives from the Old English for 'spring', and we all know about spring cleaning, whether we do it or not! Lent is a good period for spiritual spring cleaning too. As the days unfold between now and Easter, when we shall welcome the risen Lord, my invitation to you is to look around your home and consider its furnishings and fittings, and in doing so to reflect upon the furnishings and fittings of our faith. They may need polishing, repairing, sprucing up or even replacing. Furthermore, the objects of our daily lives are always with us, and we readily overlook, ignore or take them for granted. Yet they may serve as a constant reminder of our pilgrimage of faith, and we can learn to see them in a new light, enabling us to reflect afresh on God's world and our place in it.

As Lent begins, let us look around our homes in a new, spiritually creative and reflective way. And remember, today especially, that the place to start is the front door, which can be a metaphorical doorway into the period of Lent, as well as the door we open to let Christ in, so that he can rule our hearts and lead us forward in faith and hope and love.

Lord Jesus, you stand at the threshold of every heart and seek the welcome of an open door. As our doorbells invite us to welcome friends and strangers alike, may we also invite and welcome you as a permanent guest into our lives. Amen

Thursday

Threshold

Invited in

> A woman in the city, who was a sinner, having learned that
> [Jesus] was eating in the Pharisee's house, brought an
> alabaster jar of ointment. She stood behind him at his feet,
> weeping, and began to bathe his feet with her tears and to dry
> them with her hair. Then she continued kissing his feet and
> anointing them with the ointment. Now when the Pharisee
> who had invited him saw it, he said to himself, 'If this man
> were a prophet, he would have known who and what kind of
> woman this is who is touching him – that she is a sinner.'…
> Then turning towards the woman, [Jesus] said to Simon, 'Do
> you see this woman? I entered your house; you gave me no
> water for my feet, but she has bathed my feet with her tears
> and dried them with her hair. You gave me no kiss, but from
> the time I came in she has not stopped kissing my feet. You
> did not anoint my head with oil, but she has anointed my feet
> with ointment.'
>
> LUKE 7:37–39, 44–46

Yesterday, we thought about the front door and how Christ knocks
on it (or rings the bell), either as friend or stranger. Visitors to our
homes knock on the door. Sometimes they come by arrangement,
sometimes they drop by, but either way they stand on the doormat.
Before any conversation, table fellowship or other activity can take
place within the home, they must cross the threshold.

Traditionally, a bridegroom would carry his bride across the
threshold. The origins of this practice are veiled in history, but one

theory is that it derives from a fear of demons at the door who would bring bad luck if the bride tripped as she entered, and therefore she was picked up and carried in. Nowadays this is just a bit of fun, although the notion of luck is still strongly associated with marriage. Moreover, the idea that demons lurk at the door is found in the ancient tradition of blessing the home at Epiphany by chalking the initials of the magi – CMB (Caspar, Melchior and Balthasar) – on the door or doorframe. This itself reminds us of that ancient and deadly door danger, when the Israelites were told to daub the Passover lamb's blood on the doorposts to avoid the killing of their firstborn:

> Take a bunch of hyssop, dip it in the blood that is in the basin, and touch the lintel and the two doorposts with the blood in the basin. None of you shall go outside the door of your house until morning. For the Lord will pass through to strike down the Egyptians.
>
> EXODUS 12:22–23

Orthodox Jews today still put scriptures on their doorposts as a sign and reminder of whose law those in the house live by.

Being welcomed into a house by the resident is a privilege so often taken for granted. Cultural norms may encourage us to take a gift when visiting (although never to expect one!). We would expect the host to offer to hang up our coat, and we may remove our shoes for the sake of the carpets. In Jesus' day, the greeting at a door was followed by foot washing, as the famous encounter with the woman who wiped his feet with her hair reveals. Nowadays, we do not wash guests' feet or pour oil on them, but we might well kiss, hug or shake hands with them as soon as they have crossed the threshold. Not doing so might be considered rude and unwelcoming.

The threshold, often marked by a doormat inside and/or outside the actual door, is the place of welcome. Indeed, 'welcome' or some other warm greeting is often written on the doormat. As people enter our home, they are welcomed into our place of safety, in which we may take some pride, or perhaps feel shame. There are people who do not invite others into their homes because they are ashamed of how untidy or dirty it is. Others say, 'You find it as it is', and focus on the companionship of being visited.

Yet, as Simon the Pharisee was to discover, inviting people across the threshold is to court judgement. It exposes us to criticism, voiced or not, and makes us vulnerable, through the potential for report and gossip. Simon has gone down in history as the man who did not properly welcome Jesus, and who received strong criticism from his guest. It is the same for us, for while Christ stands and knocks (as we saw yesterday), if we let him in, we let in not only light but also judgement. So, if we do that at the beginning of Lent, we are exposing ourselves to the recognition that we stand judged before our Lord, who in love and mercy will look around our spiritual home and point out the errors of our ways, the dirty corners and the neglected nooks and crannies of our conscience. If we let Christ across our threshold in Lent, he will, we hope, lead us to see the faults in our faith. Yet he will not judge and leave, but dwell with us as constant guide and guardian. For we, as Jesus said:

> have already been cleansed by the word that I have spoken to you. Abide in me as I abide in you. Just as the branch cannot bear fruit by itself unless it abides in the vine, neither can you unless you abide in me. I am the vine, you are the branches. Those who abide in me and I in them bear much fruit, because apart from me you can do nothing.
>
> JOHN 15:3–5

This is to be reminded that without Christ we can do nothing. But if we let him across the thresholds of our lives, he will walk with us to the end of our days and beyond.

Father God, as we look forward to spring and Easter, help us prepare to welcome the risen Christ by self-examination, honest reflection and creative engagement with your word and the world. Amen

Friday

Fireplace

Ashes to ashes

Abraham answered, 'Let me take it upon myself to speak to the Lord, I who am but dust and ashes. Suppose five of the fifty righteous are lacking? Will you destroy the whole city for lack of five?' And he said, 'I will not destroy it if I find forty-five there.' Again he spoke to him, 'Suppose forty are found there.' He answered, 'For the sake of forty I will not do it.' Then he said, 'Oh do not let the Lord be angry if I speak. Suppose thirty are found there.' He answered, 'I will not do it, if I find thirty there.' He said, 'Let me take it upon myself to speak to the Lord. Suppose twenty are found there.' He answered, 'For the sake of twenty I will not destroy it.' Then he said, 'Oh do not let the Lord be angry if I speak just once more. Suppose ten are found there.' He answered, 'For the sake of ten I will not destroy it.' And the Lord went his way, when he had finished speaking to Abraham; and Abraham returned to his place.

GENESIS 18:27–33

Do you have a real fireplace in your home? Many houses do not these days, and few flats do. Or perhaps your fireplaces are blocked up – it is unlikely that you need one even if you have one. Yet many homes still do have a functioning grate and chimney, and an open fire in the living room has become a nostalgic, symbolic reference to an age from which we have thankfully moved on. A fire burning in the middle of the home is inefficient, dangerous and labour-intensive. Many people have replaced the open fireplace with a gas or electric fire, for reasons of safety and cost (although even these have their dangers). Nevertheless, we all know what an open fire is, and while we may not have or want one, they are still to be found in pubs, restaurants and other public places, valued and maintained for the warmth they provide and the focus of companionship they offer. (The Latin word *'focus'* means 'hearth'.)

Fire produces heat and light. The flickering flames dance with orange-hued shapes tinged with blue. In the glow, one can see and invent images and be mesmerised. You can even download videos of a flickering fireplace for the latest widescreen TVs, which in some places are installed precisely where the fireplace used to be. Something primeval is aroused in us as we sit in front of a fire, whether it is electronically created or a fire pit on a summer's evening in the garden.

Fire is neither good nor bad. Shere Khan, in Rudyard Kipling's *The Jungle Book*, calls it the 'red flower', because animals are invariably frightened by it while only humans have harnessed its power for both good and evil. Centuries ago, the pillaging of a village led to it being put to the torch; forest fires leave nothing behind; wartime bombs and terrorist explosions fling fire in our faces. Yet Louis Fieser, the man who invented napalm, also did pioneering, life-saving work on blood-clotting agents. This paradox is the paradox of fire itself, because the red flower is a beautiful, life-giving agent of rebirth as well as a dangerous flame.

The ancient Greeks told a story of the phoenix, the mythical bird that self-immolated only to rise from its own ashes, combining fear and hope in this enduring idea. High on the southern facade of St Paul's Cathedral is a statue of the phoenix rising from the ashes, a symbol of resurrection. Christopher Wren had it put there after it was recovered from the ashes of the cathedral destroyed by the Great Fire of London in September 1666. Underneath it, the word *resurgam* ('I rise') makes Wren's rebuilding of St Paul's a Christian symbol of resurrection. As well as drawing on ancient imagery, the statue makes the very building an emblem of hope and new birth for the city of London, so comprehensively destroyed by the cleansing power of fire. For it should also be remembered that the fire of 1666 purged London of the pestilence with which it had been plagued in the preceding years.

Fire burns, producing smoke and ash. It consumes everything, turning it into grey powder. For most of us, fire and ash are our body's destiny. With Abraham, we can remember that we are dust and to dust we shall return. In some churches those words are said on Ash Wednesday as ashes are smeared on the forehead in the sign of the cross, followed by, 'Turn away from sin and be faithful to Christ.' In preparation for the day, palm crosses from the previous year are burnt, reduced to grey ash for this purpose, also reminding us of the liturgical cycle of life, death and resurrection. Whether the rubble of St Paul's, the ashes of a palm leaf, the ashes in the grate at home or our own mortal remains after the crematorium has done its work, the product is basically the same: carbon reduced to ash.

Abraham knew this on two levels. First, he knew that since God intended to destroy Sodom and Gomorrah because of their extensive and rampant sinfulness, he too might be reduced to ashes along with everything else. Second, he knew that we all are but dust and ashes, inasmuch as at the end of our lives we become those. Just as what we have been is a vital part of what we are, so what we will become is also part of what we are. So it is *as* dust and ashes that Abraham entreats God to spare the city if just ten good people can be found. His own mortality and his plea for mercy are connected. This is a juxtaposition that we still find in the penitential spirituality of Ash Wednesday and the days that follow. The words used when people are marked with ash invite us to combine our remembrance of our mortality ('remember that you are but dust and to dust you shall return') with the recognition of our sinful nature and need for mercy ('turn away from sin and be faithful to Christ').

Fire is a leveller, reducing everything to the same thing. Rich, poor, large, small, animal, mineral or vegetable: fire returns them to a common substance that came into being in the first moments of creation. So, as well as being wisely frightened by fire, we are truly humbled by it. Ashes also symbolise the humility of penitence and mourning. Mordecai puts on sackcloth and ashes (Esther 4:1), and Jeremiah tells the people to do likewise (Jeremiah 6:26). Daniel and Jonah both don sackcloth and ashes as an outward sign of spiritual submission and humility (Daniel 9:3; Jonah 3:6). The modern signing with ash is a poor but powerful reminder of an ancient association. To be ashed is to be daubed with death and smothered in sin.

To return to the fireplace at home: the hearth of warmth is also the purifying place of penitence, lined with ash as it is. So, just as our earthly homes are both warmed and endangered by fire, so too are we fearful of, and grateful for, the purifying fire of God's love and mercy.

Creator God, as we stare into the flames and remember that we are but dust and ashes, help us to turn away from sin and be faithful to Christ. Amen

Saturday

Mobile phone

Take that call

Then Jesus was led up by the Spirit into the wilderness to be tempted by the devil. He fasted for forty days and forty nights, and afterwards he was famished. The tempter came and said to him, 'If you are the Son of God, command these stones to become loaves of bread.' But he answered, 'It is written, "One does not live by bread alone, but by every word that comes from the mouth of God."' Then the devil took him to the holy city and placed him on the pinnacle of the temple, saying to him, 'If you are the Son of God, throw yourself down; for it is written, "He will command his angels concerning you", and "On their hands they will bear you up, so that you will not dash your foot against a stone."' Jesus said to him, 'Again it is written, "Do not put the Lord your God to the test."' Again, the devil took him to a very high mountain and showed him all the kingdoms of the world and their splendour; and he said to him, 'All these I will give you, if you will fall down and worship me.' Jesus said to him, 'Away with you, Satan! for it is written, "Worship the Lord your God, and serve only him."' Then the devil left him, and suddenly angels came and waited on him.

MATTHEW 4:1–11

A couple of years ago, the UK government rightly decided that the previous punishments for using a mobile phone while driving were too lenient and that people were actually being killed as a consequence. A £200 fine and six penalty points on the driving licence were introduced, doubling the earlier punishment. Radio adverts were broadcast, telling people about these new penalties. After explaining the new law, the speaker declared how tempting it is to use one's phone while driving and suggested that drivers should put their mobiles in the glove compartment, saying, 'Make the glove compartment the phone compartment.' The reason, the argument went, was that the best way to resist the temptation to answer a call or text message is to put your phone 'out of temptation's way'. By hiding your phone on the other side of the car, behind a closed door, not so much the temptation to answer it as the ability to do so would be removed. So the way to handle this issue, to save a fine and 'even a life', is to put temptation out of reach. It is a good, simple idea, also effective.

According to a survey commissioned by Nokia in 2012, the average person makes, receives or avoids 22 calls a day and checks their phone every six-and-a-half minutes. Apparently, of those 22 times, we miss or avoid 16 of the calls; these are interruptions to our lives that we do not want. There is probably an age profile to this too: younger people are more attached to their phones and tend to want the latest, more sophisticated models, and they do more with them than simply make calls. Many people are wedded to their phones. Try suggesting to someone that they give up their phone for Lent and watch the look of horror spread across their face!

This is why we now need to implement preventative measures regarding what else people are doing when they are using their phones. Whether driving or operating machinery, the temptation to use one's phone while doing anything potentially dangerous needs to be avoided.

That approach – avoid temptation – sounds very Lenten, doesn't it? But it is not. If we cast our minds back to the Galilean wilderness two millennia ago, Jesus does not avoid temptation; he does not run away from it or put it in the glove compartment, where he can't reach it and it can't reach him. He does not turn his back on Satan or avoid the places where Satan lurks. Rather, he goes into the wilderness, almost seeking Satan. He goes into the devil's domain, the wilderness, where Satan arrives and starts tempting, or testing, him. In response to each temptation, Jesus quotes scripture, grounding himself and his ministry to come in Jewish tradition, spirituality and obedience. Ultimately, his response to the three temptations is threefold: trust God, obey God, worship God.

It is important to realise that these temptations do not just appear; they are not something that arise randomly for Jesus. Rather, he goes out to meet them. He goes into a situation where they will certainly arise. Then, being tempted, his divine will, determination and clarity of purpose carry him through. In doing so, he not only sets an example for us but actually succeeds for us. As in so many other ways, he has gone before us, in facing and resisting temptation and in turning the tempter's dark power to good. The outcome is that we understand that our calling, in following Christ, is to trust God, obey God and worship God. To do so involves facing temptation head-on.

What Jesus does in the wilderness is exactly the opposite of putting temptation out of harm's way. He seeks temptation, whereas we often think in terms of avoiding it. If you give up chocolate for Lent, you make sure there is none in the house. If you want to avoid the temptation to answer your phone while driving, you put it in the glove compartment or leave it behind. Yet if you want to face temptation, rather than avoid it, and thereby really grow in spiritual discipline, leave the phone on the seat next to you and make sure there is plenty of chocolate in the fridge! Just don't eat it or don't take that call. Do not make Lent easy for yourself.

We are human, and we do not necessarily need to seek temptation; it is all around us anyway. And when it comes to spiritual discipline, we can never play in the same league as our Lord Jesus Christ. Jesus' encounter with Satan in the wilderness is a *tour de force* of spiritual power and self-control. Jesus does not make it easier for himself; he makes it harder, as hard as possible. Harder, perhaps, than any human could endure. He has set us a gold standard in temptation-resistance.

May it help us but a little as we seek to honour him in this season, and strive always to answer Jesus' call to repentance and self-denial in the face of the temptation to fail to trust in God, to obey God and to worship God alone.

Jesus, as you exposed yourself to temptation in the wilderness, help us to put our trust in you and not to shy away from the issues and challenges that face us, so that we may truly respond to your call to love, serve and obey you in all circumstances. Amen

First Sunday of Lent

Mirror

Face-to-face

> Love never ends. But as for prophecies, they will come to an end; as for tongues, they will cease; as for knowledge, it will come to an end. For we know only in part, and we prophesy only in part; but when the complete comes, the partial will come to an end. When I was a child, I spoke like a child, I thought like a child, I reasoned like a child; when I became an adult, I put an end to childish ways. For now we see in a mirror, dimly, but then we will see face to face. Now I know only in part; then I will know fully, even as I have been fully known. And now faith, hope, and love abide, these three; and the greatest of these is love.
>
> 1 CORINTHIANS 13:8–13

This passage is so often read at weddings and funerals that we often think of it as a reading simply about love. When we do, we project on to the text our memories of other occasions on which we have heard it and of our experience of love shared. This builds up the picture we have created, into which the passage speaks, again and again. It is, of course, about love. The apostle Paul begins this part of his letter with 'I will show you a still more excellent way' (1 Corinthians 12:31), and then describes the way of love, trying to help the Corinthian Christians – who have a tendency to argue about what he has or has not said – to walk more surely in the new way of faith, hope and love in which their new-found Saviour Jesus Christ leads them.

Yet there is more to be reflected from the lovely stained-glass window that is this famous and shimmering text. For Paul goes on to speak of how we grow from childhood to adulthood, both physically and spiritually. In doing so, he uses the metaphor of a mirror that is both dimly opaque and mildly reflective at the same time.

A mirror needs light. In a dark room, it cannot reflect anything. Light is high-speed energy (moving about 186,000 miles per second), and when it hits something this energy has to go somewhere. There are three possibilities: it can pass through a transparent object, such as a piece of glass; it can sink in and disappear into a dark object, such as a wall; or it can bounce back off something shiny, pale and reflective, such as a mirror. Mirrors usually have a silver coating and a protective layer to prevent any light seeping through from behind. Silver reflects light well because it gives off almost as many photons of light as land on it in the first place.

The apostle Paul would just about have known of this kind of mirror, because the idea of metal-backed glass seems to have originated in Lebanon in the first century AD and the Romans made crude mirrors from blown glass with lead backings. Paul is probably thinking of such a mirror and his letter hints that they may not have been very good, producing only a dim image. It was new technology after all, replacing the polished metal mirrors used by the ancient Egyptians and Mesopotamians since around 2000BC.

In a way, unknown to Paul, the mirror itself was like a child, producing a dim image, which as time went by would be developed and improved into the fine mirrors that we all have in our homes today and, ultimately, into the mirrors that are found in space telescopes and high-definition lenses. When the mirror was a child, in Paul's day, it reflected like a child, and, as he says, produced an image that was not useful at all. It presented a bare semblance, a vague reflection, blurred and dim, only suggesting and approximating the person or object placed before it.

It is therefore important not to think of this biblical mirror as like something we have in our hallway or bathroom: the 'mirror, mirror on the wall' that can show us in detail who is fairest of them all. Paul's genius for imagery equates our knowledge of God with the dim images that new-fangled Roman mirrors were yielding, but he could also imagine what a really good mirror ought to show us. That is, what we see when we look in a mirror today is actually the kind of thing that Paul meant when he said we shall see face-to-face. For if you want to see your own face in every detail, look in a mirror, a magnifying mirror even, and you will see yourself as clearly as anyone else ever does. Nowadays, when we look in a mirror, in contrast to Paul's day, we do see what God sees: we see ourselves, warts and all.

When we look in a mirror, we do so in the hope and expectation that we will recognise ourselves. We think we know what we will see, and since most of us see ourselves each day in a mirror, we not only recognise ourselves, but probably do not notice very much. Like an artist painting a still life, we have to remind ourselves truly to *look* rather than just glance in passing or bring a particular agenda to our looking, such as 'Is my hair tidy?' We ask questions of a mirror, rather than simply letting it show us our true selves. We *see* ourselves in the mirror regularly, but do we ever truly *look*? If we do look, what do we see?

Have you ever forced yourself to look in the mirror by way of asking yourself, 'Who am I looking at?' The task each morning is to check *what* I am looking at (my hair), but when I see my face in the mirror I might ask, 'Who is that, really?'

Who are you? Who is that person staring back at you? Is that *you*? Are you a stranger to yourself? Do you actually recognise yourself in the mirror? Do you see yourself the way God sees you? (No, you don't!) Do you see a sinner, made in the image of God, in need of redemption? For just as when we read a familiar part of scripture we bring other encounters to it, other readings and experiences, when we look in a mirror in passing we see what we expect to see, what we want to see, what we have become accustomed to seeing. When we look in a mirror we usually see what we are looking for. But what we are looking for is not what God is looking for.

God is not like this. He sees us with clarity and compassion, honesty and mercy. These are the agendas he brings to his looking at us. To him, we are fully seen and fully known. In Lent, we are called to traditional attitudes of self-denial and repentance, but before we can do that the first thing we need to do is learn to recognise ourselves as the sinners we are. Without this recognition, we cannot start our Lenten – or any other Christian – journey. The word 'recognise' gives us a clue as to how to do this – we need to *re-cognise*, once again mentally and spiritually to seek to understand who we really are. To do that we need to look in a spiritual mirror, taking a good look at ourselves, but also trying to look with the eyes of our Lord, to wonder what and who he might see, really.

Father God, I am your child. Help me to recognise myself in the mirror of your mercy, and to see my face as the imperfect reflection of yours until the day when I shall truly see you face-to-face. Amen

Monday

Keys

Unlocking Lent

Now when Jesus came into the district of Caesarea Philippi, he asked his disciples, 'Who do people say that the Son of Man is?' And they said, 'Some say John the Baptist, but others Elijah, and still others Jeremiah or one of the prophets.' He said to them, 'But who do you say that I am?' Simon Peter answered, 'You are the Messiah, the Son of the living God.' And Jesus answered him, 'Blessed are you, Simon son of Jonah! For flesh and blood has not revealed this to you, but my Father in heaven. And I tell you, you are Peter, and on this rock I will build my church, and the gates of Hades will not prevail against it. I will give you the keys of the kingdom of heaven, and whatever you bind on earth will be bound in heaven, and whatever you loose on earth will be loosed in heaven.'

MATTHEW 16:13–19

At 10.00 pm every night for the past 700 years or so, the Ceremony of the Keys takes place at the Tower of London. It is a brief event but conducted with great tradition and seriousness by the yeoman warders and guards. A warder will go and lock the main gate, and on his return he is confronted by a guardsman, bayoneted gun raised, who demands 'Halt! Who comes there?' (not 'Who goes there?' incidentally). The reply comes, 'The keys.' *Whose* keys?' the soldier demands, and the warder replies, 'Queen Elizabeth's keys.' Then the guardsman says, 'Pass then, all's well', the warder and his entourage are allowed through and the brief ceremony is over in a flurry of red, black and white, and shiny boots. It is one of those British traditions of which we are so proud and which tourists love so much. Anyone can go and see it, but you have to book about a year in advance. Brief but great respect is shown to this jangling bunch of keys, which in a sense represent Her Majesty. For keys are important; they unlock things, sometimes very valuable things (these are the keys to the crown jewels, after all).

Yesterday, we saw how the Roman empire brought significant improvement into the world of mirrors, and the same is true when we consider the lock and key. Jesus, like us today, was living in a time of significant technological change. The earliest locks and keys have been dated to 6,000 years ago, to the ancient Babylonians and Egyptians. Interlocking wooden pins were operated by wooden keys, which allowed the pins to fall into place when the key was removed. An ancient example of this kind of mechanism was found in the ruins of an Assyrian palace at Dur-Sharrukin (now Khorsabad, near Mosul in Iraq and the ancient biblical city of Nineveh), dating from 704BC. Metal locks were developed centuries later by English craftsmen, but some wealthy Romans began to keep their valuables in lockable boxes at home and wore the keys as rings. As well as keeping the key literally at hand, it also showed off their wealth: not only did they have stuff worth securing, but the key itself was also valuable jewellery. When Jesus refers to keys, he may well have been referring to this recent practice of securing valuables in a locked box, with a key that was a symbol of power and wealth and was of great value in itself. To us, the key ring is what we attach our keys to, but in Roman times the key *was* a ring.

In modern times, the flat (or Yale) key, like the ones that open our front doors, was developed by a father-and-son team, both of whom were called Linus Yale. Whether or not your house keys have 'Yale' written on them, this father and son changed history in a way we barely notice. In Jesus' time, keys were a rare luxury, whereas for us now they are an essential household item, and woe betide anyone who loses them. Nowadays, one can buy a Bluetooth device to attach to a bunch of keys, so that if you do lose them you can find them using your mobile phone. Otherwise, if you lose your keys, you are locked out.

The concept of a key, however, applies not only to a physical lock. Think of the other ways in which we use the word 'key': maps and diagrams have a key; cyphers and codes have a key; there are keys on a computer or piano keyboard; there are keys on a clarinet; and the music might well be in the key of C major. The first few of these examples use the sense of unlocking something as a metaphor, as in the key to a code, whereas musical instruments and computers are using the noun to refer to something that acts physically, like opening a hole or hitting a string or making an electrical connection. Some keys nowadays do not even exist physically; they are passwords, pin codes, fingerprints or retinal scans that have replaced the physical key.

The keys that open our front doors might remind us of how we unlock our faith or, as we enter Lent, how we might unlock the doorway that leads us into this season. Just as we open our front doors with a key, how are we to enter Lent? What is the key we need? Yesterday, I suggested that the beginning of a Lenten journey is to recognise oneself as a sinner. If there is a key to Lent, it is not a literal one to unlock a door but is more like a password, like 'open sesame', to allow us authentic passage at the beginning of the journey towards the cross and beyond. The password enables us to recognise and be recognised, and it hinges on our status as sinners.

The ancient, repetitious Jesus Prayer could well be the key: 'O Lord Jesus Christ, Son of God, have mercy on me, a sinner.' This prayer combines our recognition of sin with our need of mercy, but also begins where Peter left off. The key to his being given the keys of heaven was his profession of faith, his recognition of Jesus as 'the Messiah, the Son of the living God' (v. 16). It was what Jesus needed to hear, and Peter's saying it out loud and owning the truth of it unlocked the future of the church, which has subsequently been built on this profession of faith as he articulated it. Peter's is the initial, crucial recognition of Jesus, and his being given the keys of the kingdom recognises the significance of it.

The Jesus Prayer is all you need to unlock Lent. Recognise it as such, and recognise that it is as sinners that we begin, and end, our journeys, but also that mercy can be sought from Jesus, the Son of God, and be given. Such a recognition is the key to Lent. Remember that every time you hold your keys in your hand.

O Lord Jesus Christ, Son of God, have mercy on me, a sinner. Amen

Tuesday

Safe

Storing treasure

> 'Do not store up for yourselves treasures on earth, where moth and rust consume and where thieves break in and steal; but store up for yourselves treasures in heaven, where neither moth nor rust consumes and where thieves do not break in and steal. For where your treasure is, there your heart will be also.'
>
> MATTHEW 6:19–21

Many people do not have a safe as such, but they probably have somewhere they store valuables, be it under the floorboards, hidden in a wardrobe or in some other secretive place. Yesterday, we heard about how the Romans began to develop lockable boxes in which to keep their prized possessions, locking them with metal keys that were valuable in their own right. The Romans, however, were not the first to have safes. The earliest example of a safe dates to the Egyptian Pharaoh Ramses II, who died in 1213BC. In his tomb, in the Valley of the Kings, was found a wooden safe with a locking system not unlike the pin tumbler locks in safes today. The idea was that when he arrived in eternity, all his best stuff, locked in that safe, would not have been pilfered en route. Given the amount of grave robbing that took place at the time, this approach was understandable!

The Romans developed safes that required a unique key (which made losing the key very inconvenient). During the Renaissance, wealthy people treated their safes as objects of beauty, demanding that they be ornate items of furniture as well as being secure and solid. In 18th-century England, pioneers of the modern safe were William Marr, Cyrus Price, Thomas Milner and Charles Chubb. Chubb, who died in 1845, lives on through the company that still bears his name and that epitomises security.

Jesus' injunction not to store up treasure on earth comes at the dawning of the age of locked boxes and safes. In a sense, he was telling his hearers not to get involved with creating a stash of money at home, not to sign up for this new contraption. As the Romans were developing a practical solution to the risk of theft, Jesus offered a spiritual response, saying that the stuff we value is just that: stuff. Its value is temporal; it rots, gets moth-eaten and, as everybody except the ancient Egyptians knew, you can't take it with you when you go. Jesus is telling his hearers, then and now, do not get caught up in the need to hoard treasure, but place your valuables, and your hopes, elsewhere.

Perhaps this saying of Jesus speaks to you today, as it does me, about the things you value. I have a fine piano, and recently the piano tuner opened it up and said to me, 'Get some mothballs.' For moths get inside even pianos, where they destroy the felt of the hammers and other parts, leaving behind telltale little balls of fur. Allow them to thrive unchecked, and expensive, annoying repairs will be needed. I do not have a safe in my house, but I do have a lovely piano and I do not want the moths to damage it. Indeed, it would be irresponsible of me to allow them to do so. On the other hand, the piano is just a thing – a thing of beauty and a thing that can make beautiful sounds but still just a thing. It was left to me by my godfather, and it will outlive me. Playing it, tuning it, preserving it and protecting it will not get me into heaven. This is a fact I need to recognise. We all need to recognise what we think is valuable and which of our possessions matter to us most. And then we need to distance ourselves from them. For when we do that, it will be easier to come closer to heaven, to turn our hearts and minds to storing up a different kind of treasure: a kind of treasure that moths cannot destroy.

Everything has a value these days and, while we may not have a safe embedded in the wall, our homes are like large safes, full of stuff, objects we have paid money for and things we would not want to do without. For most of us, the key to our safe is the key to our front door. Our treasure is at home, and that is where Jesus says our heart is. A Lenten journey is a venturing away from home, a venturing away from what is cosy and homely, and even if we do not step outside our front doors to do it, it is a spiritual journey in which we begin to learn to travel light. It may well give us a heavy heart to abandon the things of the world to which we are attached, but let us at this early stage begin by acknowledging that this is what we are called to do. Perhaps when we arrive at Good Friday, we will have become less inclined to stash our possessions in our safe boxes; but for now, recognition of the difficulty is enough.

Meanwhile, we might reflect on our personal safes. In a different sense of the word, there are 'treasures' stored within us, to which we cling and which we keep under lock and key. Our hearts may well be where our treasures are, but there are also treasures within our hearts. It is good to recognise what they might be. Stored in the safe boxes of our souls are experiences, memories and emotions of great love and pain alike. There are fragile, damaged and broken things locked in our hearts, and there are also flames of love and joy, flickering as we journey through life. We take care of these because they define who we are, and we know the tragedy of those who lose access to the safe boxes of their hearts through memory loss, dementia or brain injury. Our earthly existence is fragile and fleeting, so it is important to align our hearts with heaven and shepherd our inner safes to reflect our faith, our hope and our love.

Lord Jesus, you owned so little. Help us to recognise what is valuable in this life and the next, and to live as those with hearts raised to heaven. Amen

Wednesday

Hat

Hats off

> Any man who prays or prophesies with something on his
> head disgraces his head, but any woman who prays or
> prophesies with her head unveiled disgraces her head – it is
> one and the same thing as having her head shaved. For if a
> woman will not veil herself, then she should cut off her hair;
> but if it is disgraceful for a woman to have her hair cut off or
> to be shaved, she should wear a veil. For a man ought not to
> have his head veiled, since he is the image and reflection of
> God; but woman is the reflection of man. Indeed, man was
> not made from woman, but woman from man. Neither was
> man created for the sake of woman, but woman for the sake
> of man. For this reason a woman ought to have a symbol of
> authority on her head, because of the angels. Nevertheless,
> in the Lord woman is not independent of man or man
> independent of woman. For just as woman came from man,
> so man comes through woman; but all things come from God.
> Judge for yourselves: is it proper for a woman to pray to God
> with her head unveiled? Does not nature itself teach you that
> if a man wears long hair, it is degrading to him, but if a woman
> has long hair, it is her glory? For her hair is given to her for a
> covering. But if anyone is disposed to be contentious – we
> have no such custom, nor do the churches of God.
>
> 1 CORINTHIANS 11:4–16

A good friend of mine sometimes says to me, 'You can't have too
many hats.' I'm sure one can, although the poet Carl Sandburg
suggested that 'all politicians should have three hats – one to throw

into the ring, one to talk through, and one to pull rabbits out of if elected.'

Hats come in all shapes, sizes and functions, and, as is clear from the apostle Paul's comments, they are cultural objects too. As in ancient Palestine, in world cities like London, Paris and New York today, hats are a political, social and religious phenomenon. Cardinals wear skull caps, and some priests wear birettas; Muslim women may wear the hijab or burka and Muslim men the *taqiyah;* Jewish men wear a kippa or *shtreimel* and orthodox Jewish women a *tichel.*

Questions about head coverings for worship or in public take us back to the roots of all the Abrahamic faiths, to what was considered decorous by their early leaders and to what they felt the Lord required in terms of modesty and respect. The apostle Paul steps into this tradition, probably answering a question that has been asked in the newly founded Corinthian church, who are mostly Greek in cultural background. In addressing the issue of hats, he reveals and draws upon his Jewish upbringing and imports it into his teachings for the new church, saying that there is no real alternative than to follow these customs. He concludes by saying that he does not want to get into a long debate or argument about it. It is interesting that even today this issue is still contentious – for some, the forced covering of the head expresses repression; for others, modesty and decorum.

Hats are practical; they keep the head warm and dry, and enhance (or even disguise) one's appearance. The western habit of ladies wearing hats in church or at the racecourse is well-established. However, not only the wearing of a hat, but also the *kind* of hat one wears can be an indication of social status. In Elizabethan England, for example, there were clear rules about the wearing of hats or caps. In 1571, a law was passed stipulating that any male over six years old who was not a gentleman or noble must wear a woollen cap on Sundays and holy days. A hat denoted social standing, as in the scene in *Hamlet* when Ophelia comments on Hamlet's not wearing a hat as an indication of his madness: 'Lord Hamlet, with his doublet all unbraced, No hat upon his head, his stockings fouled, Ungarter'd, and down-gyvèd to his ankle… comes before me' (Act II.i.74–81). The hat that Hamlet was not wearing would have been something much posher than a woollen cap, perhaps made of taffeta or velvet. While the absence of a cap could indicate madness, its removal could be meaningful in other ways: to doff the cap was to pay respect and to hold out one's 'cap in hand' was to ask a favour.

When we put on a hat to go out into the rain or to wear on the beach to protect our heads from the scorching sun, we are ignoring these conventions, deliberately perhaps. Yet when we hold our hat in our hands, or hang it on the peg, we might remember how much cultural and religious significance we are overlooking. In the modern west, we have the freedom to wear whatever hat we want and risk only the ridicule of our friends, rather than punishment or ostracisation. (Shakespeare's uncle was fined in 1583 for not wearing the right kind of hat!) As Christians, we do not have formal practices or rules about headgear (although some denominations have conventions still), and in many places the maxim applies, particularly in relation to women, 'All may, some do and none must.' That said, generally it would not be acceptable for a man to wear a hat in church even today, and many would say that a man's hat should be removed when entering any building (except a synagogue). We have inherited conventions whereby a man wears a hat outdoors only and a woman wears a hat whenever she wants. As time goes by, these will probably become vaguer and less strict, but they still hold for now.

As we put on or remove our hats at will, we might think of our freedom. To wear a hat or not wear a hat, that is the question Hamlet did not ask. Behind the fact that we can do as we please is the freedom in Christ we have to worship and go about our business released from many of the constraints of formal religion. Renaissance, Reformation and Enlightenment history have brought us this far. Initially, we have to thank the apostle Paul, who campaigned for the right of people to become Christians without becoming Jews first. So, whether or not you wear a hat, give thanks for the freedom of faith and pray for those whose rights are curbed and denied in the name of religion, class or culture.

O God, you bring us freedom in Christ, to worship you in Spirit and in truth. Uncover our headstrong nature, and help us always to pray for those who are slaves to injustice. Amen

Thursday

Baggage

Pack your bags

> **Then Jesus called the twelve together and gave them power and authority over all demons and to cure diseases, and he sent them out to proclaim the kingdom of God and to heal. He said to them, 'Take nothing for your journey, no staff, nor bag, nor bread, nor money – not even an extra tunic. Whatever house you enter, stay there, and leave from there. Wherever they do not welcome you, as you are leaving that town shake the dust off your feet as a testimony against them.'**
>
> LUKE 9:1–5

Jesus gives this advice to his disciples twice. Here he is sending out the twelve, and then a chapter later he sends 70 more with a similar task and the same injunction: take no property, but depend on the goodwill and generosity of those whom you meet (Luke 10:1–12). The twelve are like an advance party for the 70, and this advice has been taken very much to heart by religious orders who swear vows of poverty, obedience and chastity, putting themselves at the mercy and kindness of the communities they strive to serve, unburdened by baggage. The pathway of poverty and dependence has been trodden by thousands of devout disciples over the centuries, and it still is today, by the Franciscans, for example.

Having nothing is a very challenging concept to most of us and, while we admire those who live like this, not many are called to have no baggage at all. Just as we all probably have a suitcase somewhere in the house, we all cherish our homes and our possessions. The thought of losing everything is stressful and nightmarish and, when we think of those who lose everything in a fire or in war, we shudder doubly. First, because we find it difficult to imagine having nothing; and second, we catch ourselves realising that when it comes to possessions, it is our own and others' lives that matter far more. In a similar way, when Jesus sends the disciples out, he is helping them understand that it is the job in hand, the mission of Jesus, that is far more important than belongings. They are to be living embodiments of his teaching: 'Strive for his kingdom, and these things will be given to you as well' (Luke 12:31). For belongings belong to us, but we belong to Christ.

When we make trips today, the idea of travelling light, or even going empty-handed, is very strange. Most airlines allow at least 20 kilograms of luggage, as well as cabin bags; trains have places for storing suitcases and bags; and many cars have huge boot space. Nowadays, we can travel with more stuff than the people in Jesus' day actually owned. As we shall see tomorrow when we look inside our wardrobes, throughout most of history only the rich travelled with any great amount, and even this started only relatively recently. Unless you were a great personage with a regal entourage, you travelled very light, if at all. Today, though, around a million people are in the sky at any one time (that's a whole city's worth!); in 2012, over three billion people took to the air. Travel is a big and complex business, and arguably much safer than one would expect it to be. Technology, engineering and security have made it possible to make journeys that we could hardly have imagined a century or so ago.

In Jules Verne's *Around the World in Eighty Days*, published in 1873, the main character, Phileas Fogg, does not take a bag, telling his servant Passepartout: 'We'll have no trunks, only a carpet bag, with two shirts and three pairs of stockings for me, and the same for you. We'll buy our clothes on the way.' I'm told that anyone travelling to New York to go shopping today takes the same approach, except that they buy a suitcase there and bring it back full, exchange rates notwithstanding!

Lent is a kind of journey too. In physical terms, we do not have to check in or pack clothes (or not), but each year we make a spiritual journey, and it is helpful to consider what we might wish, or need, to pack to take with us. Do we travel through Lent like Dick Whittington, carrying a few belongings bundled in a spotted handkerchief tied to a stick, following Jesus' instructions to the disciples? Or do we lug behind us a large bag with one of those orange airline tags attached saying, 'Caution Heavy'? Spiritually speaking, for most of us the latter is true.

The notion of spiritual or emotional baggage is well-known. Indeed, 'emotional baggage' has an entry in Wikipedia: 'As a metaphorical image, it is that of carrying all the disappointments, wrongs, and trauma of the past around with one in a heavy load.' A heavy load demands a strong bag, and it is likely we have one in a cupboard somewhere. Emotional baggage needs a strong bag too, and it requires us to be mentally and spiritually able to carry it. Yet not all of us are strong, and the contents of our emotional baggage can become too heavy, spill out or overwhelm us to exhaustion, causing further harm. For help, we might turn to the psalmist who tells us to 'Cast your burden on the Lord, and he will sustain you; he will never permit the righteous to be moved' (Psalm 55:22). The same Jesus who told his disciples to carry no bag also invites us, saying:

> Come to me, all you that are weary and are carrying heavy burdens, and I will give you rest. Take my yoke upon you, and learn from me; for I am gentle and humble in heart, and you will find rest for your souls. For my yoke is easy, and my burden is light.
> MATTHEW 11:28–30

These are words to cling to when hauling a heavy bag.

At home, our suitcases are empty. This is how it should be. They are ready to use, and when we next get ready to travel we will dig them out and fill them up. On our Lenten journey, we may not be able to travel as light as we want to. We may, however, be able to do the opposite of the tourist shopper; that is, to begin with a full bag and arrive with an empty one, discarding baggage as we go. This would make for a fine Lent indeed, as we resolve to throw things overboard, letting go of them on our journey and thereby lightening our load. Remember that next time you see your dusty old suitcase on top of the wardrobe.

Jesus, our burdens are so heavy and yours so light. Lighten our loads this Lent that we may walk with you, fleet of foot as we journey towards the kingdom. Amen

Friday

Wardrobe

Why worry about clothing?

> 'Why do you worry about clothing? Consider the lilies of the field, how they grow; they neither toil nor spin, yet I tell you, even Solomon in all his glory was not clothed like one of these. But if God so clothes the grass of the field, which is alive today and tomorrow is thrown into the oven, will he not much more clothe you – you of little faith? Therefore, do not worry, saying, "What will we eat?" or "What will we drink?" or "What will we wear?" For it is the Gentiles who strive for all these things; and indeed your heavenly Father knows that you need all these things. But strive first for the kingdom of God and his righteousness, and all these things will be given to you as well.'
>
> MATTHEW 6:28–33

Most people have a wardrobe with a rail and perhaps some chests of drawers. To a medieval monarch, however, a wardrobe meant something slightly different. It was a room close to their sleeping chamber in which their valuables, including their fine robes and clothes, would be kept. As it was guarded by their most trusted advisers, 'wardrobe' began to refer not only to the place and its contents, but also to the people involved. After 1200, power struggles arose between the chamber and the wardrobe, which had nothing to do with clothes but referred to access to and influence over the king. The wardrobe became a flexible powerhouse, moving around with the king. Then, in 1253, the great wardrobe came into being – 'great' because it stored large items.

Valuable commodities, such as cloth, tapestries, clothing, furniture, saddles, armour and caskets of sugar, spices, dried fruit and pepper, needed permanent safe storage and, as the older wardrobe had become more of an administrative body, the great wardrobe was created in the Tower of London. With its fixed abode, it became a place of not only storage but also the commissioning of items, and it soon outgrew the confines of the Tower. After a period of renting various spaces in the city, premises were found in what is now Wardrobe Place, near the parish church of St Andrew-by-the-Wardrobe. The armour and jewels, however, were not moved, remaining in the Tower, where they are still part of London's top tourist attraction.

Our smaller cousins of the great wardrobe, those in our houses, do not contain pepper and swords, even if they might have a fine robe or two dangling from the rail. Our wardrobes may even be a bit too full: cheap clothing, some of which is produced under appalling conditions in faraway countries where children work all day for meagre pay, abounds in the High Street. Furthermore, the amount we spend on clothes is remarkable: a survey in 2014 revealed that the 'average' British woman spends £1,200 a month on clothes, shoes and accessories, which amounts to well over half a million pounds in a lifetime. Given that there are many people who cannot contemplate such a spend, there must be many who spend far more. The wealth hanging inside some wardrobes is staggering. While some slave for the industry, others spend a fortune. Ordinary families have to budget very carefully, for children's clothing especially, because not only do clothes wear out, but also we grow and change shape. Add fashions and trends into the mix and it is easy to see how clothes join the premier league of household expense, alongside food and energy. The latter two are necessities, but while clothes are not exactly unnecessary, lack of a full wardrobe will not kill us.

Jesus said to his disciples, 'Do not worry, saying... "What will we wear?"... strive first for the kingdom of God and his righteousness, and all these things will be given to you as well' (vv. 31, 33). His words ring across the centuries, for while people have both worried about and enjoyed their clothing, there has been a great tradition of eschewing finery. Members of monastic communities have sworn vows of poverty, so that their only possession was the robe they wore. In poorer times, many people had no spare clothes. Others might have had their 'Sunday best', so called as it was, ironically, for wearing to church in a time when, as John Wesley put it, cleanliness was next to godliness and looking smart for worship was very much about both self-respect and respect for God.

Shakespeare, in a rare moment of spiritual poetry, also had something to say about what we wear. In his sonnet, 'Poor soul, the centre of my sinful earth', written around 1594, he writes about our tendency to worry about what we look like:

> *Why dost thou pine within, and suffer dearth,*
> *Painting thy outward walls so costly gay?*
> *Why so large cost, having so short a lease,*
> *Dost thou upon thy fading mansion spend?*

Shakespeare believed that the soul is trapped within the body, only to be released, and judged, when the body dies. So he places the soul at the centre of our bodies: our personal 'sinful earth'. Our sins are committed by our bodies, which we adorn and fuss over, while neglecting the inner soul, the spiritual life. We worry far too much about what we look like, spending time, energy and money on the outward appearance of something so temporal as our own bodies, which ultimately end up eaten by worms in the grave. Then, at the heart of the poem, Shakespeare asks the question, 'Is this thy body's end?' – is that it?

For sure, it is not: he goes on to encourage the reader to feed our souls, to 'buy terms divine' and to be fed within, rather than worry about the outer case that is the body:

> *Buy terms divine in selling hours of dross;*
> *Within be fed, without be rich no more:*

> *So shalt thou feed on Death, that feeds on men,*
> *And, Death once dead, there's no more dying then.*

For when the body is gone, he says, the soul lives on. Perhaps he had Christ's wonderful words of spiritual wisdom in mind: 'Your heavenly Father knows that you need all these things. But strive first for the kingdom of God and his righteousness, and all these things will be given to you as well' (vv. 32–33).

Today, charity shops have come to our aid. There are over 10,000 of them in the UK. If your wardrobe is too full or you have clothes that no longer fit you, you can take your unwanted or unwearable items to be sold cheaply or given to those in need. This, perhaps, helps those who would worry to do so less. Around half of those on low incomes use charity shops to buy clothes, which means that a real need is met, but the shops themselves do it to raise money for their causes, and so recent years have seen some of their prices rise. A careful balance needs to be maintained so that everyone benefits.

For the Christian, charity shops are a godsend, because they enable us to put these words of Jesus into action. In attempting to seek the kingdom of God, we can help others in two ways: by enabling people to buy cheap clothes and by giving the proceeds to a charitable cause that also helps others, whether through curing disease, supporting mental health or providing international aid. It is perhaps no coincidence that one of the first charity shop chains, Oxfam, has a Christian heritage. Lent is a time for spiritual reflection – for self-examination, and even for poverty, chastity and obedience. Examine your wardrobe, and see if you recognise yourself in it. What no longer suits or fits you? Give generously, sacrificially and faithfully. For these are kingdom values, and in the Lord our own needs will be met.

Heavenly Father, your eye is on all your children and you know our needs before we can articulate them. Teach us to care for the poor before ourselves, to give from our surplus and to focus on those things that clothe us in grace and peace. Amen.

Saturday

Best clothes

Zero to hero

'The kingdom of heaven may be compared to a king who gave a wedding banquet for his son. He sent his slaves to call those who had been invited to the wedding banquet, but they would not come. Again he sent other slaves, saying, "Tell those who have been invited: Look, I have prepared my dinner, my oxen and my fat calves have been slaughtered, and everything is ready; come to the wedding banquet." But they made light of it and went away, one to his farm, another to his business, while the rest seized his slaves, maltreated them, and killed them. The king was enraged. He sent his troops, destroyed those murderers, and burned their city. Then he said to his slaves, "The wedding is ready, but those invited were not worthy. Go therefore into the main streets, and invite everyone you find to the wedding banquet." Those slaves went out into the streets and gathered all whom they found, both good and bad; so the wedding hall was filled with guests.

'But when the king came in to see the guests, he noticed a man there who was not wearing a wedding robe, and he said to him, "Friend, how did you get in here without a wedding robe?" And he was speechless. Then the king said to the attendants, "Bind him hand and foot, and throw him into the outer darkness, where there will be weeping and gnashing of teeth." For many are called, but few are chosen.'

MATTHEW 22:2–14

When invited to a wedding, most people wear a suit or a posh frock. Some people go shopping specially to buy new clothes, and these clothes are not worn very often but become a sort of 'Sunday best', reserved for special occasions. Costly, attractive and of high quality, they make us feel special when we wear them. Feeling good and looking good are connected, which is why we dress up for parties, weddings and formal occasions. Underneath these clothing conventions are truths about self-esteem, hidden like psychological underwear. So, when we dress up we look good, feel good and enjoy a tiny drop of celebrity lifestyle, as we join the happy couple, the stars of the show, dressed to the nines on their big day. Whoever they are, they are the heroes of the day, and we treat them as such, rejoicing in their delightful, if short-lived, fame. This is the harmless fantasy underpinning every wedding.

Or is it? Consider the catalogue of TV hits in recent years: *Big Brother*, *Pop Idol*, *Britain's Got Talent*, *Strictly Come Dancing*, *The X Factor*, *The Great British Bake Off*, *Masterchef*. Millions lap these shows up and, if one broadcaster acquires a show from another, huge sums of money change hands and it makes national headlines. These programmes have something in common. Whatever their subject matter, they appeal to the popular idea that someone completely unknown can suddenly and instantly become famous in a single evening. This idea of 'zero to hero' means that someone especially skilled or talented but not in the public eye – the house husband who makes rather good cakes; the brilliant singer who only sings in the bath; the unknown painter, cook, comedian or ventriloquist – shoots to fame overnight.

The idea that a 'nobody' can become 'somebody' overnight is a powerful dimension of modern thought. Similarly, 'hero to zero' can also happen, as in the cases of Jimmy Saville, Harvey Weinstein and other celebrities who have fallen from public grace because of their unacceptable behaviour. 'Zero to hero' is what society believes in and fantasises about. Shakespeare hinted at this in *Twelfth Night*, when Malvolio says, 'Some are born great, some achieve greatness, and some have greatness thrust upon 'em' (Act II.v).

The garb of celebrity acquired so quickly takes getting used to, and the new-found status under the spotlight can be a real challenge. The borrowed garments of fame do not always fit and the shiny costume jewellery, glimmering in the spotlight, is shiny enough, but unreal. Some celebrities lose touch with reality and forget that hero to zero can equally quickly be reversed when they do not behave in a manner befitting the status that society has so swiftly imposed upon them. Taken from the highways and byways of the land, these new-found heroes of stage, sport and kitchen immediately find themselves in unfamiliar territory, where they are expected not only to dress but also to behave the part. When we make someone a celebrity, we expect a lot in return.

For most of us, such instant fame and celebrity is either a fiction or a pipe dream. We do not aspire to the heights of celebrity, even if we do dress up sometimes and enjoy seeing the occasional elevation of others to such social supremacy. In the parable in today's passage, we see a similar radical elevation of social status, when the master's guests decline his invitation and he sends his servants to instead invite anyone and everyone to his son's wedding feast. Here is zero to hero and hero to zero. Those who were invited to that wedding banquet, the great and the good, the official heroes, behave badly, rejecting an invitation that befits their status. They have wedding robes but refuse to get them out and wear them. So they are reduced to zero: the king destroys those murderers and burns their city.

Yet there is still the great gift of mercy, joy and salvation at the divine wedding banquet on offer, where everyone is welcomed and treated as a celebrity. The servants go into the streets and gather those they can find, both good and bad, and the hall is filled with guests. For these unexpected guests, it is their zero-to-hero moment, as greatness is thrust upon them. They are plucked from nowhere and taken to stardom, from nobody to celebrity. Except that there is a twist: in Christ, while zero to hero is absolutely possible, it is not guaranteed in this parable. One of the zeros remains a zero; he comes in but is not dressed properly, so he is ignominiously turfed out.

The scribes and Pharisees assume they have a place at the heavenly wedding feast, but scorn it by rejecting and killing the Messiah. The kingdom of heaven, originally understood to be only for the children of Israel (the heroes), is then opened up to all and sundry (the zeros). This is the work of Christ, the hero who made himself zero on the cross that we might all be heroes thereafter. This is the message of faith, that salvation came first to the Jews and then to the whole world. In this parable, Jesus is saying that those who take it for granted, for whom complacency has bred contempt, will find themselves cast out, while those who least expect it will be invited in. Heavenly celebrity status will be thrust upon them. Yet even the zeros who have become heroes must don the right robes and live up to the greatness thrust upon them. So too must we: our behaviour must reflect what we believe and, in accepting the invitation of our hero Christ to dine at the wedding feast, we recognise our own status as those who deserve zero, but, through his own self-offering and suffering, have been welcomed as heroes.

As we strive to live our lives in gratitude, humility, generosity and love, O Lord, reassure us of the greatness of your salvation that you have prepared for all believers. Amen.

Second Sunday of Lent

Shoes

Walking in hope

As for me, I am already being poured out as a libation, and the time of my departure has come. I have fought the good fight, I have finished the race, I have kept the faith. From now on there is reserved for me the crown of righteousness, which the Lord, the righteous judge, will give to me on that day, and not only to me but also to all who have longed for his appearing.

2 TIMOTHY 4:6–8

In Yad Vashem, the World Holocaust Remembrance Center in Jerusalem, under the floor in one of the rooms, visible through a plate of glass, is a pile of leather shoes, just a few of the twelve million shoes worn by those entering the gas chambers. There the shoes are now, preserved in the dilapidated, worn-out state they were in when they were carefully put down by those who either thought they were going to have a shower or knew they were not.

We all wear shoes and have done since the ancient Egyptians, and countless civilisations before them, made primitive sandals. Shoes unite us with all humankind, past, present and future, because everyone wears shoes if they can, and the history of the shoe is the history of humankind. So no one can fail to be moved by the sight of this pile of discarded shoes. They are part of, and so witness to, one of the darkest periods of human history. When the camp guards told the gas chamber victims to remove their shoes, they never dreamt that their inhuman task would yield the opposite effect and that those same shoes would end up viewed by millions as a symbol not only of how bad we have been, but also of how good we can be. Those shoes lying there, as a mournful testimony to their wearers, are also objects of hope.

All shoes are objects of hope, because they speak to us about journeys made and journeys yet to be taken. Shoes carry us forward; they are made for walking. The Holocaust shoes carried their wearers to a miserable end, but an end that will never be forgotten and which, in the years that have followed, has made those shoes haunt our consciences. For they say to us, 'Do not walk this way; do not take the path of hate and horror.'

To those who perpetrate horror and terror today, those Holocaust shoes have a message: even if all that is left after the outrage is a pile of shoes, those shoes were made for walking, and humanity will walk on, in spite of everything, because of everything. Whatever is happening around us will pass, and in 50 years will be regarded with sorrow and shame. Indomitable human spirit will triumph, and it will do so because of those who fight the good fight and run, or walk, the race of faith to which we are called in Christ. This gives us hope, as well as a warning, for we always look to the future, knowing we will be judged by the future.

We also walk in the shoes of our predecessors: those who ran the race, fought the good fight and have received their reward. Whatever path we walk, in whatever shoes, it is worth remembering that it is hopefully a long walk, and it is a walk that has a beginning and an end. No one else can walk it for you; they can lend or buy you shoes and give you a map, but in the end we walk the paths ahead of us, with all the turns, dead ends, hills and slopes that life puts in our way. The apostle Paul talks of running a race and fighting a good fight. Both are metaphors for the journey, the pilgrimage, the linear progression from the day we are born to the day we die.

Most people take an average of around 7,500 steps a day. This means that if they live to be 80 years old, they will have taken about

216,262,500 steps in their lifetime. The same average person with the average stride living until 80 will have walked approximately 110,000 miles, which is the equivalent of walking more than five times around the Earth's equator or almost halfway to the moon.

We walk almost all those miles in shoes, and the average person owns 20 pairs of shoes at any one time. Yet we are born with bare feet and we die with bare feet. Shoes are only for the journey. We meet God unshod. Moses discovered this when the Lord said to him, 'Remove the sandals from your feet, for the place on which you are standing is holy ground' (Exodus 3:5). The moment of birth and the moment of death are holy because they signify the gift of life and Christ's victory over death. Between the font and the grave, we wear shoes to carry us on our pilgrimage race, knowing that at the end we shall bare both our soles and our souls before our Lord, the righteous judge.

Lent is a time to remember this inevitable finishing line and gives us an annual opportunity to walk the course. Each Lent is a lifetime in miniature. We begin by *recognising* our frailty and our sinful nature, which we proceed to *regret* and *repent* of. Then, as we journey through the 40 days and nights, we *resolve* to *repair* our lives with the help of God, so that we may be *renewed* and at the end reach the goal of *resurrection* life. The journey through the seven Rs of Lent is a mini-lifetime, a condensed rehearsal or spiritual walk-through of the greater life we have, which itself carries us forward in hope to the eternal resurrection life we are promised in Jesus Christ. Next time you select a pair of shoes to wear, think how far they will travel, and why.

O Christ our righteous judge, we bare our souls before you in humble recognition of our need of mercy and grace. Grant that as we run the race of faith, we may find sure footing on the road you lay before us until we reach our final destination and see you face-to-face. Amen

Monday

Clock

The Lord of time

In those days Hezekiah became sick and was at the point of death. The prophet Isaiah son of Amoz came to him, and said to him, 'Thus says the Lord: Set your house in order, for you shall die; you shall not recover.' Then Hezekiah turned his face to the wall, and prayed to the Lord: 'Remember now, O Lord, I implore you, how I have walked before you in faithfulness with a whole heart, and have done what is good in your sight.' And Hezekiah wept bitterly.

Then the word of the Lord came to Isaiah: 'Go and say to Hezekiah, Thus says the Lord, the God of your ancestor David: I have heard your prayer, I have seen your tears; I will add fifteen years to your life. I will deliver you and this city out of the hand of the king of Assyria, and defend this city.

'This is the sign to you from the Lord, that the Lord will do this thing that he has promised: See, I will make the shadow cast by the declining sun on the dial of Ahaz turn back ten steps.' So the sun turned back on the dial the ten steps by which it had declined.

ISAIAH 38:1–8

Most clocks do not tick any more, but they still mark out the seconds of each minute, score the minutes against each hour and slide the hours around the daily dial, unwatched but looked at from time to time. Clocks are there to tell us the time of day, not to stand as a scoreboard of the days, months and years of our mortal lives. Yet to watch a clock is to see time itself, 'like an ever-rolling stream', carrying the hours and minutes to the sea of eternity. The hymn writer Isaac Watts used the image of a river of time, while others think of time as something eaten up.

The Corpus Clock at Corpus Christi College in Cambridge University has a large mechanical locust on top of the dial called the Chronophage (*chronos* means 'time' and *phage* means 'to eat'). As one stands and watches the clock tick away, the locust appears to devour time. It is a disturbing piece of art (unlike any of the clocks in our homes), and is deliberately inaccurate, being correct only once every five minutes, to reflect the irregularity of life. The clock was unveiled in 2008 by Stephen Hawking, possibly the world's most famous physicist. Its creator, John C. Taylor, takes the view that time is not on our side and will eat up our lives before we realise.

A similar view was expressed in the popular poem 'Time's Paces' by Revd Henry Twells (1823–1900), which was published posthumously in *Hymns and Other Stray Verses* in 1901. It reflects on what we all know to be true – that, relatively speaking, time flies as you get older.

When as a child I laughed and wept,
Time crept.
When as a youth I waxed more bold,
Time strolled.
When I became a full grown man,
Time RAN.
When older still I daily grew,
Time FLEW.
Soon I shall find, in passing on,
Time gone.
O Christ! wilt Thou have saved me then?
Amen.

The reason, perhaps, that time flies as we age is because each passing year is a smaller proportion of the life we have so far lived, so it seems shorter. Time *is* relative.

Yet time is a gift, and this passage from Isaiah tells how God decides to give King Hezekiah more of it. The gift comes with a purpose: to drive out the Assyrians from Jerusalem. Hezekiah was king of Judah during the invasion and siege of Jerusalem by Sennacherib in 701BC. This munificent gift of 15 years is vouched for by God by the turning back of the clock, or rather the passage of the sun's rays on the sundial. While today sundials are mostly ornamental, used as garden features or memorials in town squares, in the ancient world sundials were usually a reliable way of telling the time. The ancient Babylonians and Egyptians had sundials that used a vertical rod or edge (called the gnomon) to cast a shadow, which enabled the position of the sun to be read. We can suppose that Ahaz's sundial was of this kind. Later sundials employed lenses or slits to produce a line or spot of light instead. In any event, sundials present solar time at the location in which they are placed. Before the standardisation of time and the introduction of time zones, this was hardly a problem, but modern sundials need various corrections made to them so that they can reflect clock time accurately.

The story of Hezekiah's extra 15 years gives a tantalising glimpse into divine time, and no doubt makes prospective time travellers salivate. To be able to travel in time is the unholy grail of science fiction, epitomised in the TV series *Doctor Who*, the *Back to the Future* films and the adventures of numerous superheroes and villains. Ultimately (if that is a word one can use in this context!), the theory is that if one can control time and move through it at will, then the universe is at one's command. Yet here is the only example of what might be called biblical science fiction being used to explain how Hezekiah recovers from serious illness as the sundial rewinds time. We should not get too excited about this, given the relative nature of time and the inaccuracy of ancient sundials. Yet whether there are possible explanations or not, it remains the case that Yahweh, the Lord, is the true Time Lord, in whose gift is time itself.

Whether we remember that or not when we glance at the clock in the hallway or on the kitchen wall, we need not see the passing of time as a depressing death knell, constantly diminishing as the mechanical locust nibbles each blade of time. Rather, we may hear the clock ticking as the heartbeat of God's love, constant, continuous and ever-present, relentless and unstoppable. Again, as Watts puts it in the hymn 'O God, Our Help in Ages Past', a paraphrase of Psalm 90:

Before the hills in order stood,
Or earth received her frame,
From everlasting Thou art God,
To endless years the same.

As we see the seconds, minutes and hours tick away, they connect us to the divine creator, and count down earthly time at the end of which we shall be called to eternal, resurrection life, brought and bought by Jesus Christ who crossed the boundaries of time to turn the clock back on sin and offer us a new, eternal future of faith, hope and love.

God, our help in ages past and our hope for years to come, help us to see time as your gift to us with which to know and serve you on earth, until that day when there shall be no more time, only eternal resurrection life. Amen

Tuesday

Wristwatch

In sync with God

> You shall put these words of mine in your heart and soul, and
> you shall bind them as a sign on your hand, and fix them as
> an emblem on your forehead. Teach them to your children,
> talking about them when you are at home and when you are
> away, when you lie down and when you rise. Write them on
> the doorposts of your house and on your gates, so that your
> days and the days of your children may be multiplied in the
> land that the Lord swore to your ancestors to give them, as
> long as the heavens are above the earth.
>
> DEUTERONOMY 11:18–21

Most people wear a wristwatch of some kind. It might be a hand-
wound family heirloom or the latest rechargeable wonder-watch
that measures distance, heart rate and breathing while at the same
time checking emails and giving a weather forecast. The history of
the watch is not particularly ancient, the most famous early example
being a richly jewelled armlet given by Robert Dudley to Queen
Elizabeth I as a new-year gift in 1571. It is important because it was
'in the closing thearof a clocke, and in the forepart of the same a
faire lozengie djamond without a foyle, hanging thearat a rounde
juell fully garnished with dyamondes and a perle pendaunt'.

Elizabeth also had a watch set in a ring, which could scratch her
finger at a given time, serving as a kind of alarm clock. These small
clocks were driven by a spring and, while many watchmakers claim
to have invented the wristwatch, as soon as a spring-driven clock
could be made small enough, the idea of wearing it occurred to many

people at the same time, and the wristwatch was born. Generally, they were intended for ladies to wear, for men had pocket watches without straps, which could be worn in waistcoats (introduced by Charles II) and attached to chains (introduced by Prince Albert).

The keeping of time in Jesus' day was not done by anything like a modern clock or watch, but rather by the rising and setting of the sun. The day began at dawn and people went to bed at sunset. The idea of carrying time around would have been strange indeed to ancient cultures, not only because the technology did not exist, but also because the clock was in the sky, visible as stars and the sun. We who can wear time on our wrists might consider ancient timekeeping to be primitive and inaccurate, but it is only in the modern age that truly accurate timekeeping has become useful or necessary. We who can measure time by the millisecond seem to be far busier than our ancestors as a result! We can see our watches tick away the seconds and have a sense that it is our life that is ticking away with the second hand or digital counter. If we think of the ancient Jewish instruction to wear scripture on one's hand as a sign of obedience and loyalty to God's law which could not be ignored or forgotten, and which reminds the wearer who is in control of their life, then there is a modern irony in the fact that we wear wristwatches today. Do these watches do the same thing, that is, reveal what commands our life and what we live by? Are we governed and driven by time so much that we need to have constant access to it?

Jesus criticised the Pharisees for overly adorning themselves with phylacteries (see Matthew 23:5). A phylactery is a square leather case fastened by straps to the forehead. Inside it are strips of parchment on which are written texts like Exodus 13:1–16 and Deuteronomy 6:4–9. Some Pharisees and scribes had especially large phylacteries, to make a show of their legalistic devotion and thus draw attention to themselves rather than to God (we might think of watches with extra-large faces). Another kind of phylactery contained two rolls of parchment, on which the same texts were written, enclosed in a case of black calfskin. Worn on the left arm near the elbow, it had a strap to hold it in place and was called the '*tephillah* on the arm'. So, while we wear the time, they wore scripture.

There is of course no Christian command to wear a watch, but time is important as a concept for Christians, both for how we live our lives and for our anticipation of judgement and eternal life. When we put our watches on each morning, we are embracing the day, yet also submitting ourselves to its temporal limitations. We can never make a day longer or shorter, and our lives are governed by both divine and world time. The clock in the hallway keeps time for us, the alarm clock wakes us and the wristwatch makes time part of us as we wear it throughout the day, measured if not controlled by it. When we lie down we remove it, and when we rise we soon put it on. Yet it is God's time under which we live and die and enter resurrection life.

Our watches can do two other things for us. First, if we remember the wearing of scripture on the arm, we can use our watches to remind us that it is our heavenly Father who is creator of the universe and Lord of time, revealed to us in the words of scripture. The watch can represent this to us daily. In humility, we watch the seconds, minutes and hours sweep by, always aware that we are not in control, because we live in a divinely created, time-bound world. Second, on a deeper level our watches' ticking can be a constant reminder of God's presence, on hand, to guide and guard us. Every glance at our watch can be a touching base with the Lord of time. For it is the will of God we try to do and the call of Christ we try to hear, no matter how busy we are, and it is these with which we might try, at least some of the time, to synchronise our lives.

Lord of time and space, you created us and sustain us through every second, minute and hour. As we move through each day, help us to keep time with you and make time for you, that in love and grace we may follow and serve you all day long. Amen

Wednesday

Toilet

Taking away the sin of the world

> The next day [John] saw Jesus coming towards him and declared, 'Here is the Lamb of God who takes away the sin of the world! This is he of whom I said, "After me comes a man who ranks ahead of me because he was before me." I myself did not know him; but I came baptizing with water for this reason, that he might be revealed to Israel.' And John testified, 'I saw the Spirit descending from heaven like a dove, and it remained on him. I myself did not know him, but the one who sent me to baptize with water said to me, "He on whom you see the Spirit descend and remain is the one who baptizes with the Holy Spirit."'
>
> JOHN 1:29–33

Released in 2006, the cartoon film *Flushed Away* is about a pet rat called Roddy who lives in a posh London flat. One day, a rat called Sid emerges through the sewers, and after a skirmish he flushes Roddy down the toilet. Consequently, Roddy finds himself cast into a dangerous rodent underworld where there are threats at every turn, not least from the frogs and toads who despise rats and mice and want to destroy them. Naturally, Roddy and his friend Rita, who he meets along the way, survive the ordeal and it all ends happily.

It took many years of film history before anyone dared make a film that began in the loo. Yet 'flushing away' is something we all do every day and something that has been done ever since the flushing toilet was invented in Elizabethan times. Having been exiled from court for translating a naughty poem, the godson of Elizabeth I, Sir

John Harington, got back into the queen's good books by inventing the flush toilet. She was delighted and had it installed at Richmond Palace. Harington even came up with the idea of having reading material in the loo and, following the example of the queen's father, Henry VIII, who insisted that every church have a Bible chained to the lectern, Harington decided that one of his books should be chained up in every privy. He got in trouble for that too, because the book in question was a sweeping satire on court life.

A century later, across the English Channel, King Louis XIV of France often held public consultations and meetings and even took meals while he was simultaneously, shall we say, conducting other business. Two French architects, a decade apart in the late 18th century, improved on Harington's idea and the French aristocracy finally got the hint and moved from the back of the hygiene queue to the front. Interestingly, they called the new 'place' the *lieu a l'Anglaise*, and it is from *lieu* (which means place) that we get the slang word 'loo'.

While the French gave us the word, it is the British who deserve the credit for the flushing loo. Josiah George Jennings developed Harington's prototype a bit, but it was the Great Exhibition of 1851 that got things moving, for an event that attracted six million visitors merited some serious attention to a fundamental problem. Jennings installed sets of facilities, the first public lavatories since the medieval period, and charged everyone a penny. Three decades later, the famous Thomas Crapper arrived on the scene with his commercial toilets, and the rest is, as they say, history. The Deanery in Westminster Abbey still has one with his name on it.

Nowadays, we all have at least one flushing toilet in our homes, at least in the western world. The recent trend for 'toilet twinning' reminds us that outhouses and sheds are the best many people can expect, if they have proper sanitation at all. Almost 2.5 billion people worldwide do not: that is nearly a third of the world's population. Toilet twinning, if you haven't come across it, is when you make a donation to help improve the imbalance in sanitation and get a framed photo of your twinned loo to put in your own small room, to remind you of how lucky you are and to spare a thought for those less fortunate than yourself.

John the Baptist, when he saw Jesus approaching, exclaimed, 'Here is the Lamb of God who takes away the sins of the world!' (v. 29). He baptised Jesus, and so carried into Christianity the practice of ritual washing, by which sinners are cleansed, spiritually or metaphorically, something we still do regularly in our churches today. In the River Jordan, then as now, and in every font worldwide, sins are washed away, rinsed away with flowing water. This washing of the outside of our bodies symbolises the inner cleansing brought by Christ, who takes away not only my sin and your sin, but the sins of the world.

That's a lot of sin to wash, or flush, away. Yet sin is more like what we flush down the toilet than it is what we rinse off our skin; sin is not what is on the outside, but what is on the inside, so we need inner cleansing. Jesus' accusation of the Pharisees being like 'whitewashed tombs', looking lovely on the outside but dark and full of death on the inside (Matthew 23:27), applies to all human beings. We try to look good, paying attention to our outward appearance while there are darker, dirtier parts of ourselves we keep locked away, even from ourselves if we can. As with what we do in the loo, we don't talk about our sin and keep it private.

Similarly, we are reluctant to discuss such functions with our doctors, even when doing so might save our lives. We don't discuss our secret sins with our spiritual doctors much either. The old habit of regular confession has pretty much died out, except perhaps in the Roman Catholic Church. Confession is a regular motion of repentance and cleansing, flushing away all the bad stuff and entering each day renewed and refreshed by forgiveness. There is a lot to be said for some kind of daily routine that involves not only the acknowledgement of sin, but recognition of the reassurance that Jesus Christ really is the one who 'takes away the sins of the world'.

This means that, whatever we have done, there can be forgiveness. However dirty we are, inside or out, we can be cleansed by the loving mercy of God made real and present among us in Jesus Christ.

Think about that next time you pay a visit to the little room. Think about how, when you go, you are getting rid of something that you can then flush away. And remember that that is exactly what Jesus Christ does for us all, as Lamb of God and Saviour of the world.

Jesus, Lamb of God, pour down your loving mercy on me, a sinner, and help me to know that my sins can be flushed away, each and every day. Amen

Thursday

Shower

Daily ritual

Have mercy on me, O God,
    according to your steadfast love;
according to your abundant mercy
    blot out my transgressions.
Wash me thoroughly from my iniquity,
    and cleanse me from my sin.
For I know my transgressions,
    and my sin is ever before me.
Against you, you alone, have I sinned,
    and done what is evil in your sight,
so that you are justified in your sentence
    and blameless when you pass judgement.
Indeed, I was born guilty,
    a sinner when my mother conceived me.
You desire truth in the inward being;
    therefore teach me wisdom in my secret heart.
Purge me with hyssop, and I shall be clean;
    wash me, and I shall be whiter than snow.

PSALM 51:1–7

I visited a friend in America recently and, having stayed the night after a long-haul flight, awoke to find the house empty. When I ventured into the bathroom to have a shower, I found that it was of a type I had never seen before. While I worked out how to get it to produce water spraying in the right direction, I could not fathom how to change the temperature. So I had to have a cold shower. Later that day, I mentioned this embarrassing ordeal to my friend, and he immediately showed me how the shower worked and, of course, it was remarkably easy. It struck me that this was perhaps some kind of metaphor for prayer. We should all pray – we all need to pray – but so many of us do not know how to. And until someone shows us how to, prayer is like a cold shower that could, with a little guidance, instead be a warming, cleansing daily encounter with God. Like showering, prayer involves some self-discipline; it takes time (as long as you want!) and regular and often is better than weekly immersion. Weekly immersion in the bath of Sunday worship is good, and relaxing too, but a daily, invigorating dousing in prayer is best for the other days of the week.

Some people shower every day, either in the morning or before going to bed at night, or even both. John Wesley, quoting Francis Bacon, gave us the maxim 'cleanliness is next to godliness' and, since the invention of the shower, it has never been easier to stay clean. The weekly bath has given way to the daily shower, and most of us either have showers fitted over the bath or in a separate cubicle.

The first showers came directly from the heavens. One can imagine our ancestors running around in the rain to get vaguely clean, or even standing in a waterfall, but it was not until 1767 that something approximating what we would call a shower was invented. A simple technique, involving a pump that sent water into a tub suspended over the bath, enabled the bather to pull a chain, which simply inverted the tub. This remarkably unsubtle approach was succeeded in the Victorian period by a *velo-douche*, whereby the bather sat on a stationary bicycle and pedalled to produce water from above. Then came the English Regency Shower, which was very tall and by hand-pumping produced an acceptable jet. By the 1850s, indoor plumbing was possible, which meant that these tall showers could be connected to (cold) running water. Surprisingly, though, it was not until the 1960s that showering became common, and since then we have seen the advent of electric power showers and bathroom cubicles. With this ease of showering has come the hygienic ritual of a daily shower. Never in our history have we been so clean!

The shower's main purpose is the efficient and effective cleaning of our bodies. I find that a morning shower wakes me up too. A shower is part of many people's daily routine. Similarly, many people pray daily, setting aside a time and a place to do so, such as a quiet corner or in a chapel or church. While a shower can only be taken in a shower or bathroom, one can pray anywhere, but places of prayer, such as churches, do exist and it can be good to use them as they were intended. In prayer, we turn our faces upwards to God, to see and be seen by our Lord. As the living waters pour down from the heavens, we are bathed in righteousness and love. Just as the soothing water washes over us, we are cleansed, made righteous again for a new day that we have begun with confession and absolution, or rather with prayer and ablution. In prayerfully showering, we might be reminded of Isaiah 45:8:

Shower, O heavens, from above,
    and let the skies rain down righteousness;
let the earth open, that salvation may spring up,
    and let it cause righteousness to sprout up also;
    I the Lord have created it.

This could well be our daily shower prayer as we are invigorated spiritually and bodily under the warm jets of cleansing water. The shower is a manifestation of our ability to be cleansed and, just as the church has always used the idea of ritual washing to represent inner cleansing, we can be reminded of our desire and need to be cleansed inwardly every time we take a shower. Likewise, we can also be reminded of the call to pray daily: to seek forgiveness, cleansing and renewal each and every day under the pouring waters of God's mercy and love. Then we can step out into the new day, awake, cleansed, renewed, ready to welcome all the Lord sends.

Christ Jesus, you are the living water by which we are all cleansed and refreshed. Pour down your love from above, that we may be renewed in work and prayer this and every day. Amen

Friday

ßath

Wash me thoroughly

One of the Pharisees asked Jesus to eat with him, and he went into the Pharisee's house and took his place at the table. And a woman in the city, who was a sinner, having learned that he was eating in the Pharisee's house, brought an alabaster jar of ointment. She stood behind him at his feet, weeping, and began to bathe his feet with her tears and to dry them with her hair. Then she continued kissing his feet and anointing them with the ointment. Now when the Pharisee who had invited him saw it, he said to himself, 'If this man were a prophet, he would have known who and what kind of woman this is who is touching him – that she is a sinner'… Then turning towards the woman, [Jesus] said to Simon, 'Do you see this woman? I entered your house; you gave me no water for my feet, but she has bathed my feet with her tears and dried them with her hair. You gave me no kiss, but from the time I came in she has not stopped kissing my feet. You did not anoint my head with oil, but she has anointed my feet with ointment. Therefore, I tell you, her sins, which were many, have been forgiven; hence she has shown great love.'

LUKE 7:36–39, 44–47

While showers are a relatively modern phenomenon, baths are as old as the hills. In Knossos, in Crete, the water of the ancient baths came via aqueduct from the hills, and it was not necessarily cold. Where there were volcanoes, such as Santorini, dual pipe systems were installed to carry both hot and cold water into the baths. Better known are Roman baths, which employed underfloor heating, called a *hypocaust*, to waft hot air and steam into communal bathrooms. The baths in Aquae Sulis (modern-day Bath) exhibit this process very well. While everyone and anyone could bathe, men and women did not bathe together, and different classes of people tended to visit the baths at different times of day. Bathing was a social activity as well as a cleansing one, and anyone who has languished in a hot bath after a tiring day is lying in an ancient tradition. Reading in the bath is not new either: at the baths of Caracalla in Rome, built in the third century AD, there were facilities for 1,600 bathers, with two libraries. After the Romans invaded Judea in 63BC, they introduced bathhouses (also known as *hammams*), some still standing today, for example in Nablus.

Jesus would not have been familiar with the Roman bath, and in his day it was only rich people who bathed as such, while others tended to focus more on hand, face and foot-washing. King David espies Bathsheba bathing in the well-known story (see 2 Samuel 11:2–27), but this is a rare luxury, which as the wife of one of his top war heroes she can afford. The rest of the story wends its inevitably sordid and sinful way, such that it is David, in his repentance-laden psalm, who pleads with God to be cleansed spiritually: 'Wash me thoroughly from my iniquity, and cleanse me from my sin' (Psalm 51:2).

Such thoroughness was not generally available in a literal sense in Jesus' day. Instead, foot-washing was a standard activity for anyone welcoming a guest into their home. In the story of Jesus at the wedding in Cana, the large quantity of water he turned into wine (John 2:1–11) was used not for drinking but for foot-washing. People did not generally drink water, which was unhygienic; rather, they drank wine, so when it ran out there was nothing to drink. Jesus' turning water into wine was radical on every level.

Similarly, when Jesus visits the house of Simon and a woman washes his feet with tears and dries them with her hair, she is only doing what the host should have done when Jesus arrived. Or rather, what the host should have done is have a servant wash the feet of the guests as they arrived, hot and sweaty from the dusty streets. For, as Jesus himself said (John 13:10), even if one has bathed, one cannot avoid dirty feet. The feet would be rinsed with water, dried with a linen towel and then perhaps some perfumed oil or ointment applied to finish the job nicely and make the guest feel good. Foot-washing, therefore, involved not only the services of a servant, but also a degree of pampering, treating guests somewhat royally. In the story of what happened at Simon's house, we see how *not* to do this, whereas in the upper room during the last supper (see p. 171) we see Jesus doing the same for his disciples, humbly and properly.

In the 21st century, foot-washing is rare, perhaps reserved only for if one has been walking on a sandy beach in bare feet. A recent trend to immerse one's feet in a tank of small fish who nibble the toes, cleaning them in the process, seems to have been short-lived. Reflexology, and to some extent acupuncture, focuses on the feet, but for us nowadays washing is done in the bathroom, either submerged in a bath or under the running shower.

While the shower tends to be quick, efficient and perfunctory, a bath is more leisurely and, being private rather than public, gives a rare opportunity for 'me time'. A long soak in the bath gives time to think, reflect and pray: to turn 'me time' into 'we time', time to spend with God, uninterrupted by others, behind a locked door. In our modern, hectic world, the bathroom can be a place to retreat to, to shut out the noise and bustle of modern life and to indulge in one of the most ancient pastimes in a useful but extravagant way. One could say the same of going to church: much of a Sunday morning can be spent in worship and fellowship, taking up time, bathing in faith, or one might go for the spiritual equivalent of the five-minute shower. There is a place for both, and there is time for both. Invite God into either, or both, and be washed thoroughly, inside and out.

Father God, bathe me in the warm waters of mercy, that I may be cleansed from my sin and soaked in your love. Amen

Saturday

Toothbrush

Truth and wisdom about teeth

You shall give life for life, eye for eye, tooth for tooth, hand for hand, foot for foot, burn for burn, wound for wound, stripe for stripe. When a slave-owner strikes the eye of a male or female slave, destroying it, the owner shall let the slave go, a free person, to compensate for the eye. If the owner knocks out a tooth of a male or female slave, the slave shall be let go, a free person, to compensate for the tooth.

EXODUS 21:23–27

Today's passage includes one of the most famous ethical maxims of the Old Testament, one that Jesus specifically refutes, proposing instead a better way to deal with how a victim should retaliate:

You have heard that it was said, 'An eye for an eye and a tooth for a tooth.' But I say to you, Do not resist an evildoer. But if anyone strikes you on the right cheek, turn the other also; and if anyone wants to sue you and take your coat, give your cloak as well; and if anyone forces you to go one mile, go also the second mile.

MATTHEW 5:38–41

While this teaching and Jesus' undermining of it are important, we can also see how not only eyes but teeth were valued in Old Testament times. Clearly, they were of high, if not equal, significance, and the loss of one was enough to gain one's freedom. But while we might find it easy to understand how someone who had lost an eye might not be able to work as before, we might not think that the loss of a tooth would have the same consequence. After all, we have many more teeth than two.

Obviously, eyes are for seeing and teeth for eating. To have few or no teeth is a major disadvantage, and as we get older the chances of having a full set dwindle. Yet cleaning teeth is not a recent practice. When you pick up your toothbrush in the bathroom and squeeze toothpaste on to it, you are standing in a long tradition of oral hygiene. The earliest toothbrushes date from ancient Babylon and Egypt, where between 3500 and 3000BC a kind of toothbrush was made by fraying the end of a twig. Toothpaste, according to one modern manufacturer, Colgate, predates toothbrushes, and the ancient Egyptians were using it before they 'invented' brushes with which to apply it to their teeth. The ancient Hebrews, as slaves in Egypt, would have encountered and perhaps adopted the dental practices of their masters. Around 700BC, the Etruscans (northern Italians) were making replacement teeth and tethering loose teeth using gold, and the Phoenicians developed techniques using gold wire two centuries later.

By the time of Jesus, the Romans were using not only gold but also ivory and wood for false teeth, and there was legislation to ensure that if someone had gold-capped teeth they would take them to the grave, rather than pass them on to (or have them argued over by) their heirs. Investigations of the remains of volcano-hit Pompeii have revealed that the population there had good teeth, perhaps because the Romans had worked out that refined foods caused tooth decay and so recommended that rich people particularly paid attention to their teeth. The world in which Jesus lived, a mix of Greek, Jewish and Latin cultures, knew and cared about teeth, perhaps even more than his Jewish ancestors had, and Jesus' injunction not to take a tooth for a tooth may reflect the idea that deliberately removing one was not only counterproductive and mean, but also barbaric. The first-century Roman empire was a brutal, tough place, but teeth were cared for.

The earliest natural bristle toothbrushes were probably invented by the Chinese in the 15th century using pig's hair attached to a bone or bamboo handle. This was the design Marco Polo may have encountered and it is not unlike what we all use today, the first example of which was made by the Englishman William Addis around 1780. It was made of cattle bone and pig bristles, but it was not long before softer horsehair was preferred. By the late 1930s, nylon had been invented and toothbrush manufacturers have been using it ever since.

Given that very few people like going to the dentist, it is fitting that in the Judeo-Christian tradition teeth have been associated with punishment. Jesus refers to 'weeping and gnashing of teeth' seven times in the gospels, symptoms of judgement, suffering and torment associated with the end of the world. When we clean our teeth in the morning or at night (or both), we generally do not think of the end of the world, nor of judicial vengeance. However, toothache is nevertheless very painful, and the history of how it has been treated or prevented is a bloodstained, poisonous and thoroughly unpleasant catalogue of remedies that would make our teeth hurt simply to describe them. Nowadays, a swift extraction or expensive root-canal treatment are probably the worst that are likely to be inflicted upon us for our own good, and it is even possible, with due diligence and genetic good fortune, not to have to visit a dentist for many years and die old with one's own teeth still in place. Regular visits to the dentist, perhaps backed up with the occasional prayer to St Apollonia, who was martyred by having her teeth extracted before being burned alive, keep our teeth in good health.

If, as we saw two days ago, showering regularly can help us learn the discipline of prayer, then ritual teeth-cleaning is different. Showering daily is a recent phenomenon, and for centuries no one did it, nor, arguably, did they need to. But if we do not clean our teeth, they will fall out, affecting our eating, speaking and appearance. Failure to engage in a daily dental ritual brings judgement in the form of real, inconvenient and painful consequences. Failing to shower does not. That is why showering is a better analogy for daily prayer, because our relationship with God is not something that we must do for fear of punishment if we do not, but is rather a routine that yields spiritual benefits, the greatest of which is a personal relationship with God, freely entered by ourselves and rewarded with cleansing love.

Tooth-brushing is wise and prudent, and anyone who does not do it is foolish and must face the consequences. If there is a secular commandment for our age, it is 'Thou shalt brush thy teeth.' No one doubts or questions it and everyone knows the consequences – which is not to say that everyone does brush their teeth as they should, for where there is law, as the apostle Paul puts it, there is transgression (Romans 7:7–13). However, as you brush your teeth, think of the judgement that must follow from the sin of not obeying the commandments, and of the wisdom of following them. Then, as you step into the shower and recite the Lord's Prayer, think of how in Christ a relationship freely entered into bears fruit in grace, salvation and joy.

O God, you give us law and gospel to guide and teach us. May we, walking the way of your commandments, also find time to know you in your Son, Jesus Christ our Lord. Amen

Third Sunday of Lent

Spectacles

Spiritual short sight

> You must make every effort to support your faith with goodness, and goodness with knowledge, and knowledge with self-control, and self-control with endurance, and endurance with godliness, and godliness with mutual affection, and mutual affection with love. For if these things are yours and are increasing among you, they keep you from being ineffective and unfruitful in the knowledge of our Lord Jesus Christ. For anyone who lacks these things is short-sighted and blind, and is forgetful of the cleansing of past sins. Therefore, brothers and sisters, be all the more eager to confirm your call and election, for if you do this, you will never stumble. For in this way, entry into the eternal kingdom of our Lord and Saviour Jesus Christ will be richly provided for you.
>
> 2 PETER 1:5–11

Three-quarters of the world's population need to wear glasses. Over 90% of those over 65 need them. Most wear spectacles, some wear contact lenses and an increasing number are having corrective surgery, sometimes using lasers. 'Twenty-twenty vision', as the ophthalmologists call it, is not the norm but a standard, and most of us fall short, or long, of it. Such measuring of vision began in 1843. I am one of those who is short-sighted, and as I have got older I have progressed into those most clever of lenses, varifocals, which enable better distance or close vision depending on which part of the lens is being looked through. While varifocal lenses were invented in 1907, bifocals have been around since 1824 (and were attributed to the

American founding father Benjamin Franklin before that), and the first spectacles can be traced to 13th-century Italy. The first reference to using lenses for corrective vision was only two centuries earlier. This means that the writer of 1 Peter, and everyone who read it for the next thousand years, knew exactly what it was to be short-sighted but had no prospect of a remedy. When Jesus healed the blind man at Bethsaida, it was a two-stage process, and after the first stage the man said, 'I can see people, but they look like trees, walking' (Mark 8:24). Any of us who are short-sighted can relate to that; that's what I see if I take my glasses off in a busy street!

Without glasses, I could not drive, watch TV, read a poster or have an even vaguely enjoyable experience at the cinema. A large percentage of the world's population shares my ability to relate to the man who sees trees walking, and we must assume that many of our ancestors in biblical times were visually impaired to some degree. There was no remedy, it seems, and while screens and road signs were hardly there to be seen, short-sightedness was recognised, accepted and lived with as a fact of so many lives.

It is therefore interesting to notice that the apostle Peter uses such a common affliction as a metaphor for his readers' inability to see what is necessary to lead a fruitful earthly life preceding eternal life. He presents an emotional hierarchy for daily living that is founded on love. Love underpins mutual affection, which supports godliness; godliness is what enables endurance, and endurance, self-control, which fuels knowledge, which itself supports goodness, which manifests itself in faith. The list works in either direction, connecting the virtues of faith and love, and is helpful whichever way you look at it. In Peter's chain of support, love is at one end and faith at the other. Peter says that if you cannot see this, you are spiritually short-sighted, unable to see that underneath it all is the cleansing of sins we have received through Jesus Christ.

Having identified a spiritual short-sightedness, Peter offers a remedy. His corrective lenses for faith involve renewal in Christ, remembering our call in order to see the underpinnings of faith clearly. For if we can see them well enough, we will not trip up, humiliated at the gates of the kingdom, unable to see the path ahead. While we may feel that Peter's analogy of short-sightedness and blindness is harsh, given that no one could help being so or correct it, it is, however, an analogy that everyone could understand perfectly well, often from their own experience. It is hard for us to fully appreciate that most people in the first century could not see properly. Peter may not have had good sight himself, and we can surely assume that Jesus' disciples were not all blessed with 20-20 vision, even if some of them were fishermen who probably needed to see well by day and night.

Peter's corrective lenses can help us see to the heart of our faith too. If you look long and hard at your motivations, desires, purpose for living and the manner in which you go about your business, can you see a strand of love and faith that is connected by goodness, knowledge, self-control, endurance, godliness and mutual affection? Or is some of it blurred, like branches of a tree that are out of focus? Being short-sighted, do you need to look closer? Or perhaps you are long-sighted, in which case taking a step back and gaining distance can give the same benefit of clarity and focus. Either way, Peter's spectacles are helpful, and we should wear them each and every day.

When I get up in the morning, after the ritual shower and obligatory teeth-cleaning, I put my glasses on. Like everyone else who does so, it is an action I pay no attention to, and once they are on, they stay on, unnoticed. Yet I notice everything through them: if I forgot to wear them, or lost them, I would be floundering. Contemplating the history of sight-correction, I am grateful that I live in an age when poor sight is barely a disadvantage, rather than a handicapping disability. The gifts of modern science and technology, which arise from the God-given grace of human intellect and insight, are worthy of thanksgiving each and every day. So glasses are a cause of thankfulness, one lens for the literal sight of the physical eye and the other for the inner self-examination made possible through the correction of spiritual short sight.

Lord Jesus, may we never lose sight of the love that led you to the cross on which you cleansed us from our sins. Confirm your call in us that we may never stumble in faith, but rather walk in goodness, mutual affection and godliness all the days of our life. Amen

Monday

Bathroom scales

Weighed in the balance

Does not calamity befall the unrighteous,
    and disaster the workers of iniquity?
Does he not see my ways,
    and number all my steps?

'If I have walked with falsehood,
    and my foot has hurried to deceit –
let me be weighed in a just balance,
    and let God know my integrity! –
if my step has turned aside from the way,
    and my heart has followed my eyes,
    and if any spot has clung to my hands;
then let me sow, and another eat;
    and let what grows for me be rooted out.'

JOB 31:3–8

In the story of King Belshazzar's feast (Daniel 5), during the festivities he sees a hand writing on the wall, and Daniel is brought in to interpret the words. After berating Belshazzar for abusing the holy vessels that the Babylonians looted from the Jerusalem temple, Daniel translates the language on the wall. Along with the message that Belshazzar's kingship would end, Daniel reads the word *tekel*, which means 'you have been weighed on the scales and found wanting' (Daniel 5:27). The same night the prophecies come true and Belshazzar dies.

The phrase 'you have been weighed on the scales and found wanting' is one that can have a modern meaning too, which might spring to mind whenever we step on to the bathroom scales. As some predict that in the UK three-quarters of men and two-thirds of women will be overweight or clinically obese by 2030, clearly our relationship with the bathroom scales is a complex one. The scales speak the truth to us: they tell us how it is, what we weigh, and clever scales can measure our body mass index, percentage of fat or water content too, and we can track our weight using our smartphones. Many people have a kind of fatalistic attitude to their weight: 'I am what I am,' they say. Others get emotional, depressed or even ill, and there are several kinds of eating disorders that relate to responses to body weight. The humble scales in the bathroom may be a soothsayer, but as such they can be the bearers of doom and gloom, as if they were projecting judgement on to the bathroom wall: 'You have been weighed on the scales and found wanting.' 'Wanting' here means 'lacking', but many of us are hardly looking to gain what we have lost; quite the opposite!

The tradition of associating scales and balances with judgement is an ancient one. The Egyptians depicted their god Anubis weighing the hearts of the dead to see if they deserved entry to the afterlife. On the other side of the scales was an ostrich feather, which represented truth, and the soul (embodied in the heart) needed to be lighter than the feather in order to ascend to heaven. The idea that mortality and morality are connected in this way is found in many ancient cultures, and we also see it as Job pleads with God to weigh his character and so vindicate him. Job believes that only wicked people either should or do suffer, and he struggles to come to terms with the calamities poured on him when he considers himself to be just and good. He appeals to God to weigh him, seeking punishment only for what he has done wrong. The story of his ordeal is long and bleak; he is tested beyond reasonable expectation and, although he understandably considers himself to be blameless, one of the lessons of his story is that bad things do happen to good people.

Nowadays, being overweight is a bad thing, like a secular 'sin' that so many own up to but do little about. Many do not consider their body weight to be a moral issue, but it can certainly influence one's mortality. The way we behave does affect how long or healthily we live, and doctors tell us to lose weight rather as priests might say we need to confess and curb our sins. Confession leads to absolution, and crucially to the undertaking to mend our ways as best we can. Traditionally, this might be reflected in penance to help us both promise and remember to try to do better.

I remember many years ago being asked to hear the confession of a Roman Catholic lady who was committing adultery. I had never met her before, and when I asked her whether she intended to continue the relationship, she said she did. In her view she could confess it, receive absolution and carry on, planning to go to confession again in a few weeks' time. I declined to give her absolution, because forgiveness of sins is not a mechanical 'do this to get that and come again next week' operation. Perhaps I should also have reminded her of the words of Hannah: 'Talk no more so very proudly, let not arrogance come from your mouth; for the Lord is a God of knowledge, and by him actions are weighed' (1 Samuel 2:3).

Mending our moral ways and mending our physical weights are not quite the same thing, but they do have in common the connection between will and action. Sinful behaviour leads us to judgement, and requires strong will and spiritual help to rectify. It can also need a third person to challenge the sinner on the damage they are doing to themselves and others. As a postmodern, secular 'sin', being overweight also requires strong will, emotional support and the recognition that no matter how nice a person you might be, negative consequences are highly likely. The same is true of drug and alcohol abuse, smoking and other lifestyle choices that can harm us.

When we stand on the bathroom scales, we are faced with unrelenting reality. We may wish to deny or ignore it, or we may be inspired to heed a call to renewal and seek to change our behaviour. Similarly, when we submit ourselves to the loving justice of God, by standing on the scales of divine justice, we might heed God's merciful call to righteousness of life and spiritual renewal. When we stand on the bathroom scales, we are doing so for physical reasons, but we can also remember the metaphorical scales that measure our spiritual weight. Ultimately, how we respond is our choice, but we can always call on the Lord for divine help.

Heavenly Father, as our sin weighs heavy upon us, give us grace to heed the warnings of your word and your call to repent, turning around to mend our ways and return to you. Amen

Tuesday

Washing machine

They washed their clothes

When Moses had told the words of the people to the Lord, the Lord said to Moses: 'Go to the people and consecrate them today and tomorrow. Have them wash their clothes and prepare for the third day, because on the third day the Lord will come down upon Mount Sinai in the sight of all the people. You shall set limits for the people all around, saying, "Be careful not to go up the mountain or to touch the edge of it. Any who touch the mountain shall be put to death. No hand shall touch them, but they shall be stoned or shot with arrows; whether animal or human being, they shall not live." When the trumpet sounds a long blast, they may go up on the mountain.' So Moses went down from the mountain to the people. He consecrated the people, and they washed their clothes.

EXODUS 19:9–14

I remember being taught at school that Victorian children were sometimes sewn into their shirts, such that they never removed them, not even to wash. They would be split open to be removed and replaced, perhaps every six months or so. Washing clothes was an arduous task, requiring clean(ish) water and the opportunity to dry them. In an industrialised, filthy environment, cleanness was short-lived, and the standards of hygiene we take for granted today seem the more impracticable and inconceivable the further back in history we look. As recently as the 1880s, a family's washing would take a washerwoman two days, but the arrival of a hand-cranked washing machine reduced this time by half and the device only cost ten times what a washerwoman cost each week. In 1926, nearly a million such machines were sold, and housewives began to do the washing themselves. In 1937, Bendix Home Appliances introduced the first domestic automatic washing machine, although it was not until the 1950s that electric washing machines became popular in the UK and Europe. Nowadays, automatic washing machines can detect how heavy the load is and run a variety of programmes that alter the duration of the wash cycle to produce optimum results. All we have to do is put in the dirty clothes, walk away and return an hour later to move the laundry into another machine or hang it out to dry. It is a far cry from the two-day job of not much more than a century ago.

In Moses' time, clothes-washing was a symbol of cleanliness and of marking a special occasion. Moses tells the people to wash their clothes in preparation for the third day, so that when the Lord comes down the mountain they will be ready with clean garments. There are resonances here of what the angel says to John in Revelation: 'These are they who have come out of the great ordeal; they have washed their robes and made them white in the blood of the Lamb' (Revelation 7:14). Just as Moses instructed the people to wash their robes for an encounter with God, so the idea returns at the very end of the Bible. The idea of being dressed well, in freshly laundered clothes, is echoed in the tradition of wearing one's 'Sunday best'. For when we come into the presence of God, we 'present [our] bodies as a living sacrifice, holy and acceptable to God, which is [our] spiritual worship' (Romans 12:1). The metaphorical connection between sin and dirtiness is strong and ancient, finding its greatest expression in the rite of baptism, when, whether by John the Baptist or those who succeeded him, the candidate is immersed in water to be cleansed of sin. The tradition of wearing clean, white baptismal garments remains, whether the candidates are adults baptised in the River Jordan or babies in the church font.

Making our garments white is relatively easy nowadays. Soap manufacturers have special detergents for whites and many washing machines will raise the temperature to near boiling point to sterilise and clean the dirtiest of linens. Spiritually speaking, we might lament the ease with which our clothes can be washed white today. In biblical times, washing something white may well have been almost impossible, and keeping something white harder still in the dusty Middle East. TV adverts extolling the wonderful whites produced by certain detergents show that it is both possible and easy to achieve something that in the past was probably only an ideal. The washing machine makes easy something that used to be very hard, disguising the religious symbolism of washing clothes. In biblical times, it was a difficult and rare thing, requiring effort, conviction and time. As such, it was a devotional activity, demanding some sacrifice and inconvenience. The only place to wash clothes was in the river.

Yet this modern avoidance of sacrifice profoundly reminds us of the difference between Old Testament and New Testament approaches to worship and salvation. Something that was hard has now been made easy; that is, access to God and the salvation opened up for us in Christ. The Jewish law was detailed, difficult and to some extent demoralising to try to keep. As the apostle Paul put it, because there was law to follow, transgression was inevitable: 'Yet, if it had not been for the law, I would not have known sin' (Romans 7:7). However, in Christ, the law that led to sin and death is transcended by the gift of Jesus Christ and the Spirit: 'For the law of the Spirit of life in Christ Jesus has set you free from the law of sin and of death' (Romans 8:2). To put it bluntly, it is easier to be saved now that Christ has paved the way to salvation through his death and resurrection. 'It is impossible for the blood of bulls and goats to take away sins' (Hebrews 10:4), yet that is what the Israelites believed. Similarly, try as they might, they could never wash their clothes truly, sinlessly white: that can only be done in the blood of the lamb, that is, Jesus Christ.

The automatic washing machine therefore has something very profound of which to remind us – that in Christ, through his atoning sacrifice on the cross and subsequent rising on the third day, we have a new testament to salvation, a new covenant with God, a new and sin-cleansing faith, in which our washing really has been made easier, simpler and whiter than before.

We thank you, Jesus, that you have brought us a cleaner, whiter way to live, wrought through your redeeming sacrifice on the cross. Amen

Wednesday

Vacuum cleaner

Help with housework

> Now as they went on their way, he entered a certain village, where a woman named Martha welcomed him into her home. She had a sister named Mary, who sat at the Lord's feet and listened to what he was saying. But Martha was distracted by her many tasks; so she came to him and asked, 'Lord, do you not care that my sister has left me to do all the work by myself? Tell her then to help me.' But the Lord answered her, 'Martha, Martha, you are worried and distracted by many things; there is need of only one thing. Mary has chosen the better part, which will not be taken away from her.'
>
> LUKE 10:38–42

Many people do not like housework, and in the story of Mary and Martha we see two women engaged with different tasks and priorities: Mary happily listens to Jesus, while her sister Martha is rushing about doing chores that she resents. Martha's resentment causes frustration, anger even, and surely leads to stress. We feel sorry for her, for we know that in our own lives, we are likely to be living like her rather than like Mary. Martha's childlike cry of frustration, 'tell her to help me', is a heartfelt plea not only for assistance but also for justice. She feels it is not fair that she must work while her sister does not. There may even be some jealousy; perhaps Martha wishes she could be like Mary and abandon the chores to listen, reflect and learn, but something in her nature makes this impossible. Martha has a strong work ethic, such that she can only be with Jesus when she has earned the free time, while Mary is more content to see Jesus' presence as a gift and embrace it as such. Martha feels her attitude should be imposed on Mary by Jesus, but he rejects it and implies that Martha would do well to do so too, however impractical this may seem.

The further back in history we look, the longer it took to do the chores. In our age of vacuum cleaners, washing machines, spin dryers and other household machinery, not only do we not actually have to *do* the work, but the machinery does it quicker, and perhaps even better, than a mere mortal can. People of my generation used to have to do the washing-up with children; nowadays, we teach our children how to load and unload the dishwasher, a five-minute job. Even then, there can be whinging: 'It's not my turn'; 'I did it yesterday'; or even 'I don't have time'. Seventy years ago, 'washing day' was exactly that – the whole day devoted to doing the washing.

Of all the labour-saving devices, one of the most significant is the vacuum cleaner. It is a rare home that does not have one, and they come in all shapes and sizes. Recent legislation has insisted that they be made less powerful; a few years ago, one could buy a cleaner with up to 2,000 watts of power, with 1,600 watts being common. Nowadays, the power is likely to be around 900 watts. Vacuum cleaners have been using a lot of power, and the new rules are meant to save enough electricity to light 2.3 million homes a year.

The original vacuum cleaners had a similar, weaker energy rating. Invented simultaneously in Britain and the USA by Hubert Cecil Booth and David T. Kenney respectively, it was Booth who called them 'vacuum cleaners'. Both of their devices were huge and by no means suitable for domestic use. Walter Griffith's Improved Vacuum Apparatus for Removing Dust from Carpets, made in Birmingham in 1905, would be recognisable today, with its removable, flexible pipe, to which a variety of nozzles could be attached. A year later, James Kirby began designing vacuum cleaners and, in the USA, James Spangler patented the first domestic cleaner in 1908. He could not afford to manufacture it himself, so sold the patent to William Henry Hoover, whose name has been synonymous with vacuum cleaners ever since. Millions of people have been grateful for this application of science to an unavoidable chore.

Do we resent our chores or see them as a gift? The mundane task of vacuuming can, in its routine way, become an opportunity for reflection, even prayer. The monastic Benedictine tradition sees work as prayer, ensuring that time is devoted to worship, work and sleep. St Benedict (c. 480–550) himself wrote: 'Idleness is the enemy of the soul; and therefore the brethren ought to be employed in manual labour at certain times, at others, in devout reading.' The motto 'ora et labora' ('pray and work'), which has been emblazoned on much that is Benedictine since the 19th century (though it is not authentic Benedict), may help some people feel that their work is their prayer and the glory that they give to God.

For those of us imbued with what is often called the 'Protestant work ethic', this can be helpful, although it can cause us to overlook the other side of the coin, which is that life is a gift from God, so devoting time to prayer and reflection is also a good thing and not interchangeable with work. There is the work of prayer (prayer is not always easy, nor what we might choose to do at any given moment), and there is the prayer that our work may represent, especially if it is work that serves others.

Martha's work, for example, was in the service of her household and of Jesus, their honoured guest. Mary's work was to act as patient host. The two women manifest two attitudes, which can be combined in a healthy lifestyle of prayer and work: prayerful work, balanced by what some call the opus Dei ('work of God'), which is prayer and praise. We are doing God's work when we pray, and there is no reason why we cannot pray while we work and in that sense make it holy. A task that has rhythm, routine or even a ritual to it, such as vacuuming the carpet or sweeping the floor, can be a prayerful activity. George Herbert wrote in the poem 'The Temple', now well-known as a hymn:

Teach me, my God and King,
in all things Thee to see,
and what I do in anything
to do it as for Thee.

Another verse, rarely sung but also relevant, runs:

If done to obey Thy laws,
e'en servile labours shine;
hallowed is toil, if this the cause,
the meanest work divine.

This verse itself is replaced in some hymn books by this:

A servant with this clause
makes drudgery divine:
who sweeps a room, as for thy laws,
makes that and the action fine.

Nowadays, few rooms need sweeping and our drudgery is significantly reduced by the wonders of vacuum technology and dust bags. Perhaps if Herbert were writing today, he might write:

When working for an hour
on vacuuming the stair,
who cleans up dust with suction power
makes that a task of prayer.

Lord Jesus, at whose feet Mary sat while Martha worked, help us to balance our work with prayer, and so devote the thoughts of our minds and the actions of our bodies to your service. Amen

Thursday

Fridge-freezer

Ample goods laid up for many years

[Jesus] told them a parable: 'The land of a rich man produced abundantly. And he thought to himself, "What should I do, for I have no place to store my crops?" Then he said, "I will do this: I will pull down my barns and build larger ones, and there I will store all my grain and my goods. And I will say to my soul, Soul, you have ample goods laid up for many years; relax, eat, drink, be merry." But God said to him, "You fool! This very night your life is being demanded of you. And the things you have prepared, whose will they be?" So it is with those who store up treasures for themselves but are not rich toward God.'

LUKE 12:16–21

Given that the first refrigerators were invented in the 1870s, most of human history has lived without a technology that we take so much for granted today. Prior to the invention of the fridge, options for chilling food were limited; cold streams, caves or cellars had some effect, and in the winter ice could be cut. Combined with salt, some sophisticated and long-lasting storage could be achieved. The nearest thing to a fridge was the metal-lined wooden icebox of the late 18th century. Now that everyone has a fridge, these seem to us ineffective and inconvenient.

The refrigeration revolution came in 1876, when the German engineer Carl von Linde perfected a process by which liquids could be converted into gas to keep a confined space cool. Others followed, and by 1920 many companies had developed the technology to produce refrigerators, some also with freezers. Inevitably, they were expensive luxuries. As the technology developed, it became clear that refrigerators not only produced heat but also released chloro-fluorocarbons (CFCs), which, somewhat ironically, created a hole in the ozone layer, thereby helping to melt ice caps and increase global temperatures. Modern fridges have eradicated this environmentally damaging byproduct.

It is easy to forget that fridges have also eliminated famine in many parts of the world. Now that food can be frozen, it lasts longer; the medieval concept of the 'hungry gap' – the period between the food stores running out and the new crops coming in – hardly exists now-adays, except in countries whose plights we still lament on our news bulletins. Without adequate storage, food went off quickly and it was a challenge to survive the winter. Today we live in a world with not only abundant food but also the technology and infrastructure to store, transport and provide fresh, frozen or dried food worldwide. After all, we live on a planet in which frozen lamb from New Zealand can be delivered into the freezers of British supermarkets without it ever rising above zero degrees centigrade.

Food preservation, and therefore every fridge in our homes, is a matter of justice. Like the rich man in the parable, we have an abundance, and the question we ask is how to store it. In recent years, 'milk lakes' and 'butter mountains' have brought home the inevitable waste of overproduction. Market forces and pricing have created a financial climate in which it is better to waste vast amounts than to allow it to flood the market, lowering prices. Overall, there is plenty of food in the world; the problem is that some of it is in the wrong place, and not everyone is determined to see it preserved and transported to where it is needed, preferring to destroy it instead. The man in Jesus' parable does not think to *share* his bounty, but wants to increase his ability to *store* it.

As well as having literal application, Jesus' story is also metaphorical, today more so than ever. The accrual of wealth, in cash, stocks, shares and investments, is a pastime for some and a pipe dream for so many others. The distribution of money, wealth, resources and foodstuffs within communities and among nations is far from even. Yet the poor man and the rich woman, the starving girl and the spoilt boy, are all made in the image of God, loved by God, redeemed by Christ and equally called to be generous stewards of creation. Politics, religion and climate aside, there is no inherent reason why anyone *ought* to be better off than anyone else. There is also no logical reason why anyone should be paid more than anyone else, and yet the fabric of western societies is woven with uneven threads.

However wedded to the status quo of inequality we might be (and whether we like it or not), one day our life will be demanded of us; then the things we have prepared, whose will they be?

One of the ways that some people foolishly believe they can cheat death is to be cryogenically frozen. A tragic case that went through the UK courts in 2017 involved a teenage girl who wanted to be frozen at death, to be thawed and revivified later. After a legal battle with her father, she and her mother won the right for this to happen, but during the poor girl's remaining days, her mother spent all her energy fighting the case and then making preparations for her daughter's frozen body to be transported to the United States rather than spending the precious final hours with her, whose death from cancer was inevitable. The girl died alone, comforted only by the hope that one day she would be defrosted.

The fridge-freezer in the kitchen is a kind of Tardis, freezing time for a little while, so that our milk, eggs and meat will last a little longer. It is also a memento mori, a kind of coffin, delaying but not preventing decay. Everything in it has a use-by date. The psalmist asked God, 'Lord, let me know my end, and what is the measure of my days; let me know how fleeting my life is' (Psalm 39:4). Nothing lasts forever, even if our food, or our own lives, can be prolonged a little thanks to science and technology. The fridge, therefore, is a testament to the gifts of human understanding and scientific advancement, but it is also a huge, white reminder of the fact that one day we will die. Yet white is the colour of resurrection light, and it is towards that light we look – the light that reveals eternity and the God who, in Christ, not only demands our life but also gives us both earthly and resurrection life on which to build our hope.

Father God, giver of life, preserve us from selfishness, self-centredness and the desire to live forever. Help us live as those whose compassion and generosity spring from the assurance of resurrection hope. Amen

Friday

Kettle

Boiling point

O that you would tear open the heavens and come down,
  so that the mountains would quake at your presence –
  as when fire kindles brushwood
  and the fire causes water to boil –
to make your name known to your adversaries,
  so that the nations might tremble at your presence!
When you did awesome deeds that we did not expect,
  you came down, the mountains quaked at your presence.
From ages past no one has heard,
  no ear has perceived,
no eye has seen any God besides you,
  who works for those who wait for him.
You meet those who gladly do right,
  those who remember you in your ways.

ISAIAH 64:1–5

While we may take for granted that most British kitchens have a kettle, it is not necessarily the case in many other countries. In Britain, we love a cup of tea, and tea needs water to be almost boiling – experts say black teas are best at 85°C, white and green teas at 70°C and herbal teas at boiling point. According to the appliance manufacturer Russell Hobbs, the first electric kettles were introduced by Compton and Co in 1891. Early kettles were inefficient, and it was not until 1922 that Swan introduced a kettle with an internal heating element. These could boil dry, and it was Bill Russell and Peter Hobbs who invented the automatic kettle in 1955. Whatever the rights and wrongs of boiling water for tea (for coffee it should not be boiling), it is worth remembering the scientific adage that the boiling temperature of water is 100°C at sea level; that is, the scientific fact is relative to location. So, for example, my Italian friends who live in Mexico City tell me that their spaghetti takes a few minutes longer to cook since they moved there (Mexico City is 2,240 metres, or 7,380 feet, above sea level, and many visitors initially experience some degree of altitude sickness). So when Isaiah asks God to come down from the heavens and cause the mountains to quake, the boiling point up there would be lower than at ground level!

Isaiah is not joking, of course; he is deadly serious. His prayer of penitence that precedes this passage is in earnest and is made on behalf of God's people, who have not only erred and strayed from God's word and laws but have also been justly punished, such that they feel abandoned in the face of enemy assault and deprivation. Isaiah pleads for God to make himself known in terrifying power to those who are 'his' adversaries. It is a heartfelt plea that echoes across the centuries among any people who feel abandoned, unjustly treated or both. At the same time, it is troubling because, as in some of the psalms, Isaiah is wanting retribution and suffering to be wrought on his people's enemies, whom he takes to be God's enemies too. Isaiah wants God's boiling anger to be visited on those who persecute his people, and it can be tempting to pray for retribution on those who cause suffering or for the downfall of one's enemies. Yet vengeance is the Lord's (Romans 12:19), and the history books are a catalogue of one revenge wreaked on another, as are the great works of literature, such as Shakespeare's *Romeo and Juliet*, which shows the futility of feuding.

Humanity – capable of devising technology to boil water in a kettle using energy extracted from the wind, minerals and nuclear fission – has also used every resource to wage war in a spirit of anger, hatred, malice and fear. It is not the technology itself, but the purposes for which it is developed and the use to which it is put. Boiling can produce steam for sterilising needles for life-saving operations, or it can heat oil into a terrible weapon. In our homes, we know that boiling water, useful as it is, is dangerous. As we saw with fire (see p. 16), boiling water is to be treated with care and attention; yet a cup of tea is one of life's most soothing and restorative drinks.

Our ancestors in faith would have known this dichotomy in their relationship with God. Isaiah and his fellow prophets were quick and keen to point out that it is the same God who loves and judges, who provides for his people but also imposes hardship, military defeat, exile and famine when his people err and stray from law and worship. With the smooth comes the rough, and the message of the prophets often involved admonishing the population and entreating them to return to the Lord. God could and would boil with anger, but he could and would also soothe and restore in response to contrition and praise. While there was an understanding that sometimes God's judgement was inflicted through the invading armies of the Assyrians or Babylonians (for example), here Isaiah is pleading not only that God would show his face to his faithful people in mercy and relief but also that, in relieving their burden, he would show his face as the God of victory to their enemies and detractors.

It is all too easy for Christians today to dismiss this kind of view as Old Testament judgemental anachronism, and blithely say that no one still believes in a God who behaves in this way or who can be addressed in this manner. Many say that the God who smites or smiles from on high has been replaced by a loving God of mercy, who in Christ seeks the salvation of all through Christ's self-offering, atoning sacrifice, which removes our sins and paves a path straight to the embrace of God. Yet neither this domestication of New Testament gospel nor the decisive dismissal of the Old Testament God of judgement is entirely accurate, helpful or even reflective of current attitudes worldwide. For today, there are still many of all faiths who desire God to boil against enemies or who feel that they are on the receiving end of his wrath. Recent controversies in the English-speaking church about the popular hymn by Keith Getty and Stuart Townend, 'In Christ Alone', in which the reference to God's wrath annoys some, reveal that the balance between our understanding of God's love and his righteous anger has by no means been settled. Similarly, the question begged by Isaiah in this outburst, as to whose side God is on, is still controversial, as we see religiously motivated wars raging around us now. It is just as easy in our day and age to paint God as we want him to be: on *our* side; hating *our* enemies; and rather like us, to make it a bit easier for us to be like him. Yet God is not a kettle to switch on at will, to boil at those we want him to and to soothe us with like-minded love.

Next time you put the kettle on, remember that love and judgement go hand in hand, and they always have done. Pray for those who believe that vengeance is theirs not the Lord's, and remember all who suffer from the religious zeal and intolerance of others who presume to act in the name of God.

Pour down your mercy, O Lord, on all who beg for relief and repent of their sins. Disown those who kill and maim others in your name, and teach us all to fear your judgement and live in your love. Amen

Saturday

Electricity

Power in the storm

Early in the morning [Jesus] came walking towards them on the lake. But when the disciples saw him walking on the lake, they were terrified, saying, 'It is a ghost!' And they cried out in fear. But immediately Jesus spoke to them and said, 'Take heart, it is I; do not be afraid.'

Peter answered him, 'Lord, if it is you, command me to come to you on the water.' He said, 'Come.' So Peter got out of the boat, started walking on the water, and came towards Jesus. But when he noticed the strong wind, he became frightened, and beginning to sink, he cried out, 'Lord, save me!' Jesus immediately reached out his hand and caught him, saying to him, 'You of little faith, why did you doubt?' When they got into the boat, the wind ceased. And those in the boat worshipped him, saying, 'Truly you are the Son of God.'

MATTHEW 14:25–33

Between 1975 and 2007, Toronto's CN tower was the world's tallest free-standing structure, at just over 553 metres high. It is still one of the world's highest buildings. CN stands for Canadian National, the railway company that built it, and the tower is used for telecommunications and broadcasting. It is also a tourist attraction, and visitors to the tower can ascend in an elevator to the top and admire the stunning views of the city and Lake Ontario. In part of the viewing gallery floor is a slab of thick glass on which one can stand and look down nearly 500 metres to the earth below. Standing on it is like floating in mid-air, with nothing beneath your feet.

It is strange being suspended between heaven and earth like this, and when I was up there I could not bring myself to step out on to that glass-covered void. 'O me of little faith!' I say, because I know that standing on that plate of glass is perfectly safe. Thousands, if not millions, of people have done so already, and no one has ever fallen through.

Yet knowing something to be safe and being able to take a step of faith even in the face of evidence are quite different. Rather like the apostle Peter seeing Jesus walking on the water, there is hard evidence that something that seems impossible *is* possible, but our inherited fears conflict with what is before us, and we have to replace fear with faith. Peter is therefore to be admired for his faith on seeing Jesus walking on the water, for he steps out in confidence and is borne along, saved from sinking by his faith. But then when the storm comes, he gets frightened, has doubts about what he is seeing or doing and begins to sink. Just as his faith saves him, his doubt causes him to sink. Rather than sink or swim, however, he calls on Jesus, who takes his hand and saves him. Peter may well have been able to swim, but in a storm that would not have been good enough; he could not have saved himself.

We are seldom faced with this kind of challenge. Yet every and any day our faith may be tested, not only spiritually but also scientifically, so to speak; for we trust science and technology too, albeit in a slightly different way. Take electricity: without some faith in the theory and practice of electricity, we would become paralysed by fear, rather like Peter was. Do you understand how electricity travels around your home, and how dangerous it can be?

Interestingly, Peter the fisherman might have known about electricity, as there are records dating to the ancient Egyptians that refer to electric fish, and the Romans knew that electricity could be conducted through water as a predatory device employed by rays and catfish. Peter might have known that water and electricity do not mix well, even if electrocution was the last thing he feared when walking on the waves. Nevertheless, the history of the discovery of electricity did not really begin until around 1600, and it was the 19th century that saw major developments in understanding, such that during the 20th century electricity became a household necessity and the huge electricity-generation industry burgeoned. Wind farms, hydroelectricity, solar panels and nuclear power have slightly reduced our climate-damaging dependence on coal and gas, to keep charged the electric circuits running around our homes, which we can literally plug into.

The single-phase electric power that runs through our walls carries alternating current between the power grid and the household, and is usually earthed, to prevent damage from lightning. Circuit breakers and fuses are also there to protect us, lest there should be a surge or other problem, and we rarely pay attention to them unless one breaks or blows. We take electricity for granted and yet, through error or misfortune, it causes house fires, explosions and electrocutions. While we 'trust' the electricity flowing through our house, if we paused to think about it, we might become very scared. What would someone from Peter's age think and feel, walking into a modern house, seeing something that kills other fish in the water being used to power lights, appliances, communications and entertainment systems? It is easy to forget both how remarkable and how recent this all is. And it is all ultimately powered by the natural world that God created, even if we have become over-consumers of that world in order to increase our own desire for power.

Peter had insufficient faith in what he could see; he doubted and so began to sink. Even though he initially trusted, because walking on water contradicted everything he took for granted, he floundered and had to be rescued. For us, who do not get the opportunity to walk on water (even if we can stand on a plate of glass 500 metres above ground level), we can find that what we have believed in, often for years, is buffeted by a storm and we begin to consider what underlies our faith: we think about whether what we believe really adds up. If we did that with electricity, we would be frightened to turn anything on and would have to sit in the dark. Yet, whether our trust in electricity is shaken or not, it continues to work; it is there, nevertheless. If a circuit is broken, it can be mended.

Perhaps there are short circuits in your faith. Perhaps some fuses have blown and the power is not getting through. What you need is an electrician. What we all need when we are sinking, or when the fuses are blown, is a renewed encounter, in the heart of the storm, with our Lord Jesus, the spiritual electrician of our buffeted souls. His call and his hand of help are offered and outstretched amid the short circuits of despair and the raging waters of self-doubt.

Jesus, you call us over the tumult of our life's wild, restless sea; day by day your sweet voice sounds, saying, 'Christian, follow me' (adapted from 'Jesus calls us, o'er the tumult' by Cecil Frances Alexander).

Mothering Sunday

Family photos

Who is my family?

> While he was still speaking to the crowds, [Jesus'] mother and his brothers were standing outside, wanting to speak to him. Someone told him, 'Look, your mother and your brothers are standing outside, wanting to speak to you.' But to the one who had told him this, Jesus replied, 'Who is my mother, and who are my brothers?' And pointing to his disciples, he said, 'Here are my mother and my brothers! For whoever does the will of my Father in heaven is my brother and sister and mother.'
>
> MATTHEW 12:46–50

Our attitude towards, and use of the word, family is not as straightforward or consistent as we might think. It is easy to assume that our family is made up of wife, husband, children, parents, aunts, uncles, siblings, cousins, nieces, nephews and, by extension, in-laws. These are all to be found in the 'Table of kindred and affinity' found in the *Book of Common Prayer*, which defines who may or may not marry whom. As such, it has become a sort of definition of who is 'in' a family, but that was never its intention, nor is it accurate, then or now.

The diarist Samuel Pepys (1633–1703) described his family as including not only his wife but also his servants. The origin of this use may lie in the fact that the Latin word *famulus* means a slave, and *familia* indicates ownership of someone. The head of the household was not considered to be a member of the family but the one to whom they were all subservient. Shakespeare reminds us in *Romeo and Juliet* (which is about two 'families'), that one's family included everyone under the same roof, whereas it was one's 'friends' who were the blood relatives. Nowadays, the words have almost been reversed, although some organisations are beginning to use the word 'family' as a friendly, inclusive way of describing a group of people with a common interest who love and look after one another. In this way, we can speak of the Scouting family and, as in many communities, the church family.

The idea of the modern 'nuclear' family (two parents and one or two of their own children) has expanded in recent years to accommodate a broader norm that reflects a greater prevalence of divorce, remarriage and partnerships outside marriage, such that the interrelationships between members of a single household are much more fluid and disparate, and collections of stepchildren and step-parents cohabit in various permutations. The widening of the concept of marriage in many countries introduces another dimension and, while there is controversy about whether 'marriage' must involve a man and a woman, no one disputes the use of the word 'family' to describe the core of relationships created under the home roof that also extends to a wider network of relations. More so than ever, families come in different shapes and sizes and are defined by a variety of considerations – love, friendship, kinship, money and convenience.

A glance at any of the family photographs in your home may confirm this range of possibilities. Every family has its stories and anecdotes about members past and present, and has its things that are talked about and not talked about, which could be matters that are scandalous, tragic, painful or, of course, funny. Every family member has opinions about every other family member, and the family photo album serves as an aide-memoire, speaking to us of affection and happy memories. The pictures also provide the impetus for family storytelling, and this encourages and builds up the sense of relatedness among family members, past and present. This is especially true as family members learn to recognise their ancestors and distant relatives, connecting them to the bigger picture of the wider family – their stories, lives and relationships. Modern technology aside, this is hardly a new practice: Matthew opens his gospel with a lengthy account of Jesus' genealogy, which tells us that it mattered to first-century Palestinians as much as it does to us today who your parents were.

If we combine this phenomenon with the commandment to honour one's father and mother (Exodus 20:12), we then see Jesus' apparent rejection of Mary and her children as quite revolutionary. Whether or not we take the view that Jesus had (step)brothers and sisters (born to Mary after his own birth), there is certainly a family unit active here. Moreover, the absence of Joseph or any other paternal figure in the scene could mean that Mary is a widow, which makes Jesus' dismissal even worse.

On the other hand, we need not see this incident as Jesus disowning his family, but rather as Jesus redefining the notion of family, and being neither the first nor the last to do so. Remembering that we are to some extent imposing a modern definition – the 'nuclear family' – on to the concept, we may see in this scene that Jesus is highlighting and affirming new bonds of connectedness that are based not on kinship but on common purpose, affection or service. Jesus' words have influenced Christian living ever since, and it is very much in the spirit of the 'family of those who seek to do the will of God' that churches speak of the 'church family' today: a group of people who gather under God's roof in love and learning, worship and work for the kingdom. Nevertheless, the church – the *ecclesia* – are those who gather together to be sent out into the world with the gospel, *ek clesia* meaning 'called out'.

This is a long way from the ownership that we found in Samuel Pepys' 'family'. Yet we do own our friends and loved ones in the best sense of the word, and in having portraits of them we extend our relationship to include them in their absence, even beyond the grave. The choice as to whose portrait or which wedding photo adorns the mantelpiece or sideboard is ours, and as often as not we see reflected in the photograph the faces of those we love, associated with events we cherish. The camera is a mirror with a memory, and in the faces of family photos we form and continue inner fellowship with the living and the dead, just as our ancestors and their families did with paintings. Yet we are also members of Christ's family, striving to do his Father's will, united as such with all the saints, some of whom we may even have portraits of at home.

God of love, whose son Jesus Christ shared the family home in Nazareth, draw the whole human family to yourself, and grant that all human families may dwell in love and peace and mutual care, always. Amen

Monday

Keepsakes

Throwing and gathering

For everything there is a season, and a time for every matter under heaven:
  a time to be born, and a time to die;
  a time to plant, and a time to pluck up what is planted;
  a time to kill, and a time to heal;
  a time to break down, and a time to build up;
  a time to weep, and a time to laugh;
  a time to mourn, and a time to dance;
  a time to throw away stones, and a time to gather stones together;
  a time to embrace, and a time to refrain from embracing;
  a time to seek, and a time to lose;
  a time to keep, and a time to throw away;
  a time to tear, and a time to sew;
  a time to keep silence, and a time to speak;
  a time to love, and a time to hate;
  a time for war, and a time for peace.

ECCLESIASTES 3:1–8

When someone dies, his or her possessions are distributed around the family, sold or thrown away. Many of us have keepsakes of loved ones acquired in this way. Increasingly, we have so much stuff in our homes that when they have to be emptied, for whatever reason, there is a great deal of sorting out to be done. 'Stuff' is an interesting word with various meanings, ranging from the filling inside an object such as a teddy bear or cushion to the more modern meaning of just about everything and anything. We might say, 'Have you got your stuff?' or 'Let's put your stuff in the car.' Where we used to say 'things', now we say 'stuff'.

Whatever we call our stuff, we certainly have a lot of it. We have a lot of stuff, we throw away a lot of stuff (not quite in equal measure, I suspect) and it may well be that we have a lot of stuff that we ought to throw away, too. As the writer of Ecclesiastes puts it, there is 'a time to throw away stones, and a time to gather stones together' (v. 5). Yet what we have thrown away can come back to us too: in Lyme Regis in south-west England, there is a waste mountain created around 50 years ago that has crept closer to the sea due to coastal erosion, and now the former rubbish dump is shedding its treasures on to the beach. Archaeologists are sifting through the junk, reclaiming, examining and cataloguing the 'stuff' they find – old cookers, sinks, the kind of things that were thrown away in the 1950s. It is worth remembering that in the 1950s people did not have anything like as much stuff as we do now.

There is a time to throw stuff away, and there is a time to gather things. 'For everything there is a season, and a time for every matter under heaven' (v. 1). The unknown writer of Ecclesiastes is claimed by some traditions to be King Solomon, while others associate the book with King Hezekiah (see 'Clock', p. 54). Whoever the author is, their observation in today's passage about there being a time for everything has struck a chord with readers over many centuries. The pop song 'Turn! Turn! Turn! (To Everything There is a Season)', written by Pete Seeger (1919–2014) quotes this text verbatim. Popular as it is, there are stings in some of its tails, for there is recognition here that war, dying, plucking up, destroying, throwing away, killing, breaking down, weeping, hating and tearing all have their place in the great picture that makes up human existence. Whether that place is rightful is not in question, but no one can deny that these unsavoury flip sides of love and laughter are real and ever-present.

One of the ways in which we handle the realities of death, grief and loss is to gather keepsakes, things that remind us of someone or, because they belonged to that person, retain something of them for us. We cannot keep the dead with us, but an ornament, item of clothing or tool acts as something more than a souvenir, taking on deeper significance. After a funeral, friends of the deceased may be invited to have something of theirs, as a memento. Other things, from jewellery to musical instruments, are passed down through the generations. Who the past owner of an object is can be more important than the object itself or its function.

There is a time to gather such objects and, according to Ecclesiastes, a time to let go of them too. When someone has died, the disposal of clothes in the wardrobe, toiletries in the bathroom or the favourite old chair can be difficult, and it may not be able to be undertaken immediately. Some people preserve loved ones' bedrooms as shrines to their memory, unable to touch any personal items. Yet the time may come to move on, to 'throw away stones', even those that have memories embedded in them. For others, those stones are far too heavy and cannot be lifted, let alone cast away.

We might wonder, then, what stones we have gathered – that is, mementoes or keepsakes that can or should be kept or discarded. The time to discard them might not be now or it might be never, but when we examine our keepsakes we can both think of them for what they *are* and also reflect on what or who they *represent*. When we hold one in our hand, we think of the lost loved one (some might even say we pray for them), but just as we know there is a time to die and a time to be born, we know that they, unlike the memento, are gone. So the keepsake emphasises that they are gone, but also helps us keep their memory alive.

As with the contrasts listed in today's passage, so our remembering and our forgetting are linked. There is, as the writer might say, a time to remember and a time to forget. A keepsake helps us do both at the same time and helps us handle our grief and move forward as one season gives way to another.

Christ Jesus, you are remembered in the breaking of bread; help us remember with gratitude and acceptance all those whom we love but see no longer, ever mindful that nothing can separate us from your love. Amen

Tuesday

Calendar

Day by day

What gain have the workers from their toil? I have seen the business that God has given to everyone to be busy with. He has made everything suitable for its time; moreover, he has put a sense of past and future into their minds, yet they cannot find out what God has done from the beginning to the end. I know that there is nothing better for them than to be happy and enjoy themselves as long as they live; moreover, it is God's gift that all should eat and drink and take pleasure in all their toil. I know that whatever God does endures forever; nothing can be added to it, nor anything taken from it; God has done this, so that all should stand in awe before him. That which is, already has been; that which is to be, already is; and God seeks out what has gone by.

ECCLESIASTES 3:9–15

Every year, in time for Christmas, my wife and I make a calendar for our family and friends, with a family picture above each month and the dates on the calendar marked with not only the major days of the year but also some ecclesiastical dates (such as Ash Wednesday) and the various birthdays of members of the family. We have been doing this since our daughter was born, so these calendars, which most people have kept over the years, have become also a record of her growing up. These calendars are tailor-made by an online company, so inevitably are unique to us.

Every year we mark our birthdays, and with increasing age we make less of them, although we sometimes pause to celebrate the milestone ages, often with a mixture of pleasure and poignancy. For time waits for no one, and the relatively modern marking of anniversaries and birthdays is, metaphorically speaking, a double-edged sword. Many years ago, seasonal festivals were observed more so than birthdays, and that practice seems to be returning – a stroll down any high street reveals that the celebration of birthdays has been subsumed into the rollercoaster of special days that runs through every year – except that religious festivals have been mostly supplanted by dates on which to celebrate mothers, fathers, grandparents, dead people (Halloween), helping others (Red Nose Day) and so on. There is nothing wrong with this: it simply serves to keep our calendars full as we are propelled through the year with annual events to remember, commemorate, celebrate, mark and spend money on. Mammon has developed a liturgical cycle too, and card and gift shops follow it religiously.

As well as telling us how many days to next Sunday there are, or what date to write at the top of the page, our calendars remind us of which secular, religious or family festival is approaching. As we near someone's birthday or wedding anniversary, we may think of them and perhaps pray for them (some churches do that each Sunday); at the very least we remember them, and they become a focus for us, if only for a day or two.

Some calendar dates are written in for us, printed nicely on the calendar itself, while others we write in ourselves as appointments that we and others might need to remember to keep. As well as calendars, some people have diaries, printed or electronic, into which they enter the schedule of their upcoming life. Some people have very full diaries, while others have no need of a calendar, being so lonely that every day seems the same and to mark their passing is too much of an agony. Do you sigh with relief to see a day in the calendar that is empty, or do you long for more events in your diary?

Calendars speak to us of human interaction: appointments to keep, invitations to accept, dates to remember that relate to friends and family. Calendars keep us busy as well as record how busy we are. A full calendar indicates a network of relationships, with others and with God – another kind of calendar is the liturgical calendar. Christian communities have observed holy days (holidays) for centuries, and the 'calendar' is the list or chart of when they fall and whose feast day they instruct us to commemorate.

Liturgical calendars are still in use today, and contain two kinds of holy day: those which always fall on the same date, such as Christmas (25 December) and All Saints' Day (1 November); and those driven by the date of Easter, such as Good Friday and Pentecost (50 days after Easter). Some of these dates are moveable, either so that they do or do not fall on a Sunday, or because of Easter-related festivals. A saint's day cannot fall on Good Friday, for example, and so must be transferred to a nearby date. The date of Easter itself is complex and appears to be swathed in mystery, but in the western church always falls on the Sunday following the first full moon after the vernal equinox (21 March). All these dates in the church calendar remind us of the story of our faith, and the accompanying lectionary tells us what scripture to read and say together; they instruct and invite us to come together to mark the day. Communities that live and pray together have extensive liturgical calendars to follow *because* they meet together. At the same time, the calendar is an invitation to meet together to pray and share fellowship. Calendars are all about relationship, whether or not they have photographs of family members on them.

The writer of Ecclesiastes gives a sobering perspective on the busyness of our lives and the tendency to be guided, even ruled, by calendars or diaries. For no matter how busy we are, or how full our calendars, time marches on; everything we do, or plan to do, or have done, needs to be placed in perspective against the eternal, divine time of God. Astrophysicists tell us that before the Big Bang there literally was no time, and that there may yet be a context in which there is no more time. This is not so different from the idea that the 'end of the world', however nigh it is, will transform time and space into something else, something incomprehensible to us here and now.

Our calendars map out our little zone of time, keeping us busy, but are almost meaningless in the great scheme of things. However, this is not something to be depressed about; rather, it is something to be humbled by. When we see our calendar on the wall, headed by the year and month, and perhaps with a nice picture too, we see our lives in detail, but we can also be reminded that 'whatever God does endures forever; nothing can be added to it, nor anything taken from it; God has done this, so that all should stand in awe before him' (v. 14). So we can stand before our calendars in awe of God, under whose creative, loving gaze everything 'which is, already has been' (v. 15); that which is yet to happen, is already happening; and, perhaps even more profoundly, that which we consider to have happened in the past, is still real. God seeks out the past, present and future simultaneously. For God the Trinity is not only three persons in one, but also past, present and future, three times, in one.

O God of the Trinity, you hold all the dimensions of space and time in your hand. Help us both live for the moment and in eternity, so that whether we are busy or lonely, we may be always sustained by you. Amen

Wednesday

Radio

Tune in and transmit

> Then the Lord spoke to you out of the fire. You heard the sound of words but saw no form; there was only a voice. He declared to you his covenant, which he charged you to observe, that is, the ten commandments; and he wrote them on two stone tablets. And the Lord charged me at that time to teach you statutes and ordinances for you to observe in the land that you are about to cross into and occupy.
>
> Since you saw no form when the Lord spoke to you at Horeb out of the fire, take care and watch yourselves closely, so that you do not act corruptly by making an idol for yourselves, in the form of any figure – the likeness of male or female, the likeness of any animal that is on the earth, the likeness of any winged bird that flies in the air, the likeness of anything that creeps on the ground, the likeness of any fish that is in the water under the earth.
>
> DEUTERONOMY 4:12–18

The idea that a voice could be heard with no visible source hardly bothers us today, but it would have confounded the 18th century. In biblical times, it was a symptom of divine interjection. When Moses or the apostles Peter or Paul heard a voice, it was overpowering and incontestable (see, for example, Exodus 3:4–6; Acts 9:4; 10:13). Nowadays, those who hear voices are likely to be diagnosed with schizophrenia, even though the voices they hear are real to them. Yet, whenever we turn our radios on we hear voices, and music too. This does not concern us, for we know how it works and admire those who have made it possible for one person to speak to a nation. During World War II, radio came into its own, and the famous broadcasts of King George VI, Neville Chamberlain and Winston Churchill informing Britons of the state of war and its progress are milestones in radio history. It is fascinating to contemplate how far radio technology has come in the last century and how ubiquitous radios now are. Kitchens, lounges, bedrooms all have them, and many of us are woken up each day to the sound of words but see no form, and think nothing of it. Radio signals can be beamed to us from outer space, and in recent years analogue radios have been complemented by digital radios. Peter and Paul would have been amazed, and probably quite frightened!

Many people believe that the radio was invented by Guglielmo Marconi (1874–1937), but this is not quite true. Like so many whose names have become synonymous with inventions, his work built on that of others. As early as the 1820s, pioneers such as André-Marie Ampère and Michael Faraday were experimenting with electromagnetism and it was James Clerk Maxwell (1831–79) who first suggested that electromagnetic waves could be used for communication. David Edward Hughes made the first electromagnetic transmission around 1880, while Heinrich Rudolf Hertz did a similar thing, for which he is famously remembered for believing his experiment had little practical value! Far from it: the development of radio technology was then picked up by Marconi, although it was Reginald A. Fessenden who was the first person to send a radio message, on 23 December 1900, and the first ever public radio broadcast, on Christmas Eve 1906. That was around 3,200 years after Moses heard God's voice at Horeb, and 1,870 years after the apostle Paul walked to Damascus.

Moses and Paul heard commandments: Paul was told to stop persecuting Christians, while Moses was given instructions to avoid idolatry. The lack of form of God causes caution: God cannot be formed out of clay, metal or wood, and so can only be thought of as a disembodied voice, unlike the idols that existed in other cultures at the time. The words and love of God are spoken and transmitted through living beings, not works of human craft. Human beings are not themselves to be worshipped, though, but rather the words of God they transmit are to be honoured and revered.

Religious broadcasting aside, we do not generally hear the voice of God on the BBC, or any other station for that matter. Some stations, such as Premier Christian Radio, broadcast material exclusively for the faithful; BBC Radio 4 has its Sunday and daily worship slots and Radio 3 still presents Choral Evensong from a cathedral or musically resourced church. How long these broadcasts will continue remains to be seen and heard.

Radio listening has become an individual activity, whereas in the early days it was much more communal. A family or household would gather in the main room to 'listen with mother' or hear the news, but over the past half-century such listening has become a solitary activity. A glance around any railway carriage will reveal passengers connected to phones, iPods and radios. When those people get home, they may well watch TV alone too, while perhaps other members of their family watch or listen to something else on another device.

The intrusion of sound into the rooms we inhabit is something we choose to allow, and many people have the radio or TV on as a kind of companion, or to keep the children entertained. Many do not actually pay attention to it; it is just on. I have many times paid a pastoral visit to someone, be it an older person or the family of a baptismal candidate, to find the TV on, and it has remained on throughout the conversation I have attempted to hold. When I have asked for it to be turned off, some people have said they did not notice it was still on and some may even seem offended that I asked.

On the other hand, George Orwell's dark vision in *1984* of a society in which every room has a 'telescreen' that not only plays content, but can also see what is going on has almost become real. Orwell wrote his novel in 1948, inverting the digits to get the year of his dystopic future and, while his vision has not come to pass as such, internet technology can put cameras and microphones almost anywhere, and in the service of personal safety we welcome technology of which Orwell would have been deeply suspicious.

Meanwhile, we may firmly believe that God is watching us in some sense, or at least watching out for us. But God does not spy on us. God is more like a constant companion, not so much broadcasting to us, but speaking to us in our inner beings, through the presence of the Holy Spirit in our lives. Sometimes it is easier to tune into this than at other times. We cannot see God, yet we can hear him, and by the Sprit we can feel his love transmitted *to* us, and others can feel God's love transmitted *through* us. In a sense, we are all transmitters, radios of redemption, living and speaking of God's redeeming love revealed in Jesus Christ's life, death and resurrection. Just as Moses transmitted the commands of God to the Israelites in the wilderness, Christ's disciples broadcast his gospel. Since the time of Jesus' commission, recorded at the end of Matthew's gospel – 'Go therefore and make disciples of all nations, baptizing them in the name of the Father and of the Son and of the Holy Spirit, and teaching them to obey everything that I have commanded you' (Matthew 28:19–20) – we his followers have continuously sought to obey it, remembering always that he is with us, to the end of the age. So it is for us and our calling, to tune in and transmit the love of Christ to all.

Jesus, as the sound of your mercy goes out into all the world, help us to be the transmitters of your love, joy and peace. Amen

Thursday

Television

Here's looking at you

[Jesus and his disciples] came to Bethsaida. Some people brought a blind man to him and begged him to touch him. He took the blind man by the hand and led him out of the village; and when he had put saliva on his eyes and laid his hands on him, he asked him, 'Can you see anything?' And the man looked up and said, 'I can see people, but they look like trees, walking.' Then Jesus laid his hands on his eyes again; and he looked intently and his sight was restored, and he saw everything clearly. Then he sent him away to his home, saying, 'Do not even go into the village.'

MARK 8:22–26

Television lets us see the world through new eyes. What we see affects our lives; it can dismay and depress us or drive us to prayer. It can lift our spirits, make us laugh or cry, and teach and inform us. It can show us life, from birth to death, and can connect us to momentous events of joy and sorrow. The age of TV, while it may be passing, has built new kinds of national and international communities, held together not by faith or politics but by what aerials and transistors beam into people's homes. News from afar comes crashing in on us: famines in Africa; storms in the Americas; floods in the Indian subcontinent; terror attacks in Europe; earthquakes in Asia and New Zealand. We expect to see pictures and be told everything within minutes of an event, and it is the TV culture that has made it possible. Twenty-four-hour news channels fuel a demand and supply the desire for constant information, and they drip-feed news into the bloodstream of social media and the always-on internet. We do not need to go into the village for news now; it is beamed to us constantly, and our TVs can tune into it all day and night.

Television and radio are obviously connected, sociologically and technologically. Once the ability to transmit radio broadcasts was mastered, TV was inevitable. The first TV broadcast was transmitted from Alexandra Palace on 26 August 1936, and began with Leslie Mitchell saying, 'Good afternoon, ladies and gentlemen. It is with great pleasure that I introduce you to the magic of television.' Then followed a song, specially written by Ronnie Hill, called 'Here's Looking at You', sung by Helen McKay. All this happened not that long ago – many people still remember the advent of television and there are plenty more whose childhood did not involve much or any TV. It is often said that Queen Elizabeth II's coronation in 1953 gave the impetus for many people to acquire a TV, and others gathered around their neighbours' sets to see the pageantry of that momentous occasion. The picture quality, and for some the reception, was poor, and the images may well have resembled 'trees walking', but an exciting new age was dawning, and it was only going to get better, just as it did for the blind man of Bethsaida.

Television has changed the way we grow up, that is, how we learn, are taught, spend our leisure and play time, and experience the wider world around us. Consequently, this affects the way we see the world and think about things. It has opened our eyes in so many ways and superseded other avenues of exploration and adventure. TV, like so much of technology, is in itself morally neutral, but the ways it is used and the ways we allow it to show us things and speak to us can have significant consequences. The same can be said of its offspring, the internet, which now provides so much choice and on-demand content that the garden-variety TV set is already evolving into something far more agile.

Some things, however, do not change. Recall that in the Bible images are associated with idolatry, specifically condemned as anathema to a monotheistic faith. Leviticus 19:4 says succinctly: 'Do not turn to idols or make cast images for yourselves: I am the Lord your God.' This commandment relates to statues, but we do not have to look far for modern equivalents. An idol is something that distracts us from the worship and reverence of God, and today we have the opportunity for and susceptibility to idolatry in so many ways, most of which are manifested on our TV sets. The word 'idol' has become an accepted description for someone who has many fans and, now that social media has introduced the world to 'followers', we find ancient religious concepts transferring their meaning. My idol may be a pop star or footballer, and I can 'follow' them (and 'friend' them) on social media. Recall that Christianity rejects idols and calls us to follow Christ, who calls his followers 'friends' (John 15:15).

In the TV age, our graven images are moving ones, darting across the screen with alluring, pixelated glory. TV is a wonderful invention, a companion to some even, but we must always be on our guard against the idolatry and manipulation it can promulgate. As well as admiring the clarity of digital imagery and sonics of surround sound, we must not let our sight be blurred into blind acceptance of what is presented, nor become a slave to TV schedules, trapped in the ongoing sagas of soap operas and constant news feeds. There is a wide world out there, and the moral ambiguity of TV is that we can allow it to both introduce us to that world and prevent us from engaging with it. If you get too close to a TV screen the images look blurred, so it is important to keep a good distance to get good focus. Like the blind man of Bethsaida who saw trees walking, we need clarity, and that comes with distance. Just as Jesus told him not to go into the village where he would have become an instant focus of attention, gossip and interpretation by the locals, we too need to maintain a healthy and faithful distance, reflecting on what we see, in order to, as they say, see the wood from the trees.

Lord Jesus, help us to see the world through your eyes. By your Spirit, transmit to us your compassion and truth, that as we watch your world we may see the Father's love revealed in all creation. Amen

Friday

Computer

Wiping the dead heart

> I will take you from the nations, and gather you from all the countries, and bring you into your own land. I will sprinkle clean water upon you, and you shall be clean from all your uncleannesses, and from all your idols I will cleanse you. A new heart I will give you, and a new spirit I will put within you; and I will remove from your body the heart of stone and give you a heart of flesh. I will put my spirit within you, and make you follow my statutes and be careful to observe my ordinances. Then you shall live in the land that I gave to your ancestors; and you shall be my people, and I will be your God. I will save you from all your uncleannesses.
>
> EZEKIEL 36:24–29

Most of us have something that runs on a computer chip and that also contains some kind of hard disk. Computers certainly do, needing a hard disk to store the operating system and the documents, emails, information, passwords, settings, images, music files and other digital material we accumulate. Now that the days of floppy disks are gone, a hard disk is essential. Nevertheless, it can fill up, get damaged, become corrupted, cease to work or just go dead.

That happened to me recently: the hard disk in a backup drive I used stopped working, so I removed it to see if I could make it work. No success; the disk was dead and the data on it inaccessible. So I bought a new disk, formatted it and got my backups up and running again. My precious documents, such as the books I have written for The Bible Reading Fellowship, are safe and sound!

The problem, though, is what to do with the old hard disk. All the best advice says that one should not simply throw a broken or non-functioning hard disk into the rubbish bin. Not only is it recyclable to some extent, but there is always the chance that someone might get hold of it and somehow restore or otherwise access the data, and that data might be sensitive or private. It may not actually matter whether anyone else gets hold of our old emails, photos and documents, but bank details and passwords are worth protecting.

If the disk still works, you can write blank data over what is there and sell, give away or reuse the disk. It takes a while, but it is easy to do. It is much harder if the disk does not work. According to a website I found, there are ten ways to destroy a disk (none of which are ideal!): burn it, but this releases toxic fumes; shoot it; remove the powerful magnets and platter inside; smash it with a hammer, being careful of broken glass and flying metal (best to wear safety glasses); put it near a huge magnet, like the ones at car scrapyards (ordinary magnets are not powerful enough); crush it with an industrial crusher (the author Terry Pratchett left instructions in his will that his hard disks should be run over by a steam roller); melt it with acid (wear protective clothing); microwave it (needs to be done outside and may destroy the microwave too); drill holes in it and cut it up with an angle grinder; or finally, use water and sodium bicarbonate on it to generate electrolysis. Having read these instructions, I just put my old disk drive in a box and put it in a cupboard, not being brave or foolish enough to attempt any of these approaches!

Hard disks, while seemingly fragile and even temperamental, are very difficult to destroy completely. Sitting at the heart of our personal computer, smartphone or TV recorder, hard disks store our personal details and secrets: financial records, letters, notes, photos, songs and so on. They can, therefore, be thought of as a virtual repository of our lives. We might variously think of the hard disk as like the brain, the heart or the soul. The disk, however, is simply the storage device; it does not make things work as such (that is the CPU), so it does not really equate with the brain. The computer is not dead if you remove the hard disk, although it would not work. Yet, as anyone who has lost a disk knows, it stores data that gives us access to our memories, relationships, hopes and aspirations, and to our own personal and family histories and stories. To lose one's electronic data is upsetting, stressful and frustrating.

When Ezekiel was living with and preaching to the Jewish exiles in Babylon in the sixth century BC, they too were feeling disoriented, frustrated and despondent. The Lord appeared to have deserted them, and the fact that King Nebuchadnezzar II had had 3,000 Hebrews deported from Jerusalem to Babylon felt like divine punishment in two senses: they had been ripped from the heart of their homeland, and their heart had been ripped from them as they struggled to sing the Lord's song in a strange land, as Psalm 137 famously puts it. Their memories of the past and their hope for the future, along with their possessions and networks of relationships, had been disrupted. What they needed was new spiritual hard disks, new hearts of flesh, to replace the seized-up, sinful ones of 'stone'. Damaged and dirty, deserted and doleful, the exiles needed rejuvenation, restoration, resurrection even. Later, Ezekiel uses the imagery of dry bones being breathed back to life (Ezekiel 37:1–14) as an image of restoration that points us both backwards to the suffering of exile and forwards to the resurrection of Christ.

Just as we can replace the corrupted hard disk in our computers, God can give us a new heart of flesh to replace the solid, dead heart of stone. Doing so involves wiping away sin and being cleansed of idolatry, backsliding and rejection. The new heart that God gives is blank, like a new hard disk, ready to have the law of the Lord written on to it and a new spirit of loyalty and love bestowed upon it. Such is the renewal in Christ that comes through having our sins washed away; through having our dead hard disk wiped clean; through having a heart of stone replaced with a heart of flesh. All these metaphors speak of the renewing power of God, who can make what is dirty, clean; what is corrupt, healthy; and what is damaged, repaired. There is no need to smash our soul with a hammer, to immolate it or to drown it in a bath of acid; rather, we can be cleansed and refreshed by the living water of the Lord, putting new life into that which was damaged and dead.

Next time your computer plays up or the hard disk goes kaput, remember that we too can be wiped clean and restored, and that it is not necessary for God to utterly destroy us, for he can and will restore and renew what is broken, enabling anyone to start afresh, any time.

Lord, you know the secrets of our hearts and the uncleanness of our souls. Wipe our hard hearts with the loving mercy you have revealed in Jesus Christ, so that we may be refreshed, restored and renewed. Amen

Saturday

Pen

Mightier than the sword

O that my words were written down!
O that they were inscribed in a book!
O that with an iron pen and with lead
they were engraved on a rock forever!
For I know that my Redeemer lives,
and that at the last he will stand upon the earth;
and after my skin has been thus destroyed,
then in my flesh I shall see God,
whom I shall see on my side,
and my eyes shall behold, and not another.
My heart faints within me!
If you say, 'How we will persecute him!'
and, 'The root of the matter is found in him';
be afraid of the sword,
for wrath brings the punishment of the sword,
so that you may know there is a judgement.

JOB 19:23–29

Before we had computers and speech-recognition software, we had pens (and still do!). The art of pen-making is a fine one, and good pens can fetch high prices. Most people would accept that a computer costs around a thousand pounds but would think it extravagant, even profligate, to spend that kind of money on a pen. Yet the pen is one of the most valuable inventions of humankind; it is one of the most powerful tools we have. Everyone should know how to use one, and to be denied the right to do so is an injustice many tyrants have discovered. A pen is an instrument of freedom and of self-expression, a purveyor of truth and a spinner of lies, and one strike of its sharp nib can bring death and destruction to individuals and communities. The pen, as the playwright Edward Bulwer-Lytton put it in his historical play *Richelieu* in 1839, is mightier than the sword.

Of course, the pen of itself has no moral value whatsoever, any more than a computer or knife does; it is what it is used for that matters. History has taught us that the potential of a pen for good or evil is very great, so a pen is one of the most potent artefacts one can possess. Whether it is a cheap biro or a diamond-encrusted, handmade designer fountain pen we hold in our hand, doing so connects us to almost all of history. The armistices of 1918 and 1945 were signed with a pen; as were the death warrants of Mary Queen of Scots, King Charles I and Louis XVI; as were the Tudor Act of Succession, the Treaty of Versailles and the formal notification of the UK's intention to withdraw from the European Union. Luther penned his 95 theses in 1517 and the first Magna Carta was handwritten and then sealed in 1215 (it was not actually 'signed' as such by King John; rather, he placed his seal upon it). The British Library in London has on display some of the most significant documents in history, almost all of which are handwritten. Among these is the original manuscript of Handel's *Messiah*, in the composer's handwriting. Usually, the book is open at the page of the 'Hallelujah' chorus, arguably the most famous piece of choral music ever written.

If you were to turn over that page, you would find an aria written for a solo soprano entitled 'I know that my redeemer liveth'. It is almost as famous as the preceding chorus, and its text is, perhaps surprisingly, not from the gospels but from the book of Job. This passage is also often read at the burial of ashes; usually, several weeks after a funeral has taken place comes the opportunity to bury the remains of a loved one, perhaps in an urn, with a small gravestone to mark the plot. These words, which speak of one's name being inscribed in a book and of a stone being engraved with an iron pen, are poignant, as in my parish church and many others there is a register of who has been buried and where. An engraved stone marks the spot, recording at least the name of the deceased, and the dates between which they breathed the air of planet earth.

It is an iron pen that Job desires and, while he sees its ability to carve a name into rock, we might also think of Jeremiah's complaint: 'The sin of Judah is written with an iron pen; with a diamond point it is engraved on the tablet of their hearts' (Jeremiah 17:1). Nowadays, it is easier to engrave stone (it can be cut with a laser using a design on a computer), but the plea, and the desire underlying it, are still the same: 'O that my words were written down!' (v. 23).

Job is not generally associated with hope. His story is about how God allows Satan to taunt and torment him, heaping upon him numerous sufferings and trials, yet, through it all, he will not relent and curse God. Today's passage comes as part of Job's response to his so-called friends, who goad him to give up on God. Job will not, nor does he ever do so, in spite of the hideous sores and discomforts that are heaped upon him. Rather, he declares that he knows his redeemer lives and that on the last day, even after his body has decayed, Job will see him face-to-face. For he believes in justice, in the reward of heaven and the consolation of eternal hope.

Job is an example to us all. His desire for an iron pen to write with lead in the stone is the opposite of writing in the sand. With Job we know, like the psalmist, that:

> As a father has compassion for his children,
>   so the Lord has compassion for those who fear him.
> For he knows how we were made;
>   he remembers that we are dust.
> As for mortals, their days are like grass;
>   they flourish like a flower of the field;
> for the wind passes over it, and it is gone,
>   and its place knows it no more.
>
> PSALM 103:13–16

Rather than write our words in the sand, we might, like Job, yearn for an iron pen, so that even though our bodies blow away as dust, the words we have spoken and written and the deeds we have done might be remembered from one generation to another.

Salvation, while it can be attested to in pen and ink, is not to be found in the words on the page, but in what is written on the heart. For 'the steadfast love of the Lord is from everlasting to everlasting on those who fear him, and his righteousness to children's children, to those who keep his covenant and remember to do his commandments' (Psalm 103:17–18). Those commandments were themselves written on tablets of stone, yet, as words, they only make up part of the picture. For the redeemer to whom Job looks in hope is Jesus Christ, the Son of God and the incarnate Word, written on the page of time for evermore. It is he in whom we put our trust, he who has no gravestone, he whose passing through death into resurrection life writes the story of our future hope and our names in the book of life (see Revelation 20:11–15). He is our redeemer, whom we shall see on the last day.

Jesus our redeemer, God's only Son, write your words of mercy on the tablets of our hearts, that we may know ourselves to be saved and so put our hope in you. Amen

Passion Sunday

The Bible

Do you understand what you are reading?

Now there was an Ethiopian eunuch, a court official of the Candace, queen of the Ethiopians, in charge of her entire treasury. He had come to Jerusalem to worship and was returning home; seated in his chariot, he was reading the prophet Isaiah. Then the Spirit said to Philip, 'Go over to this chariot and join it.' So Philip ran up to it and heard him reading the prophet Isaiah. He asked, 'Do you understand what you are reading?' He replied, 'How can I, unless someone guides me?' And he invited Philip to get in and sit beside him. Now the passage of the scripture that he was reading was this:

'Like a sheep he was led to the slaughter,
    and like a lamb silent before its shearer,
        so he does not open his mouth.
In his humiliation justice was denied him.
    Who can describe his generation?
        For his life is taken away from the earth.'

The eunuch asked Philip, 'About whom, may I ask you, does the prophet say this, about himself or about someone else?' Then Philip began to speak, and starting with this scripture, he proclaimed to him the good news about Jesus.

ACTS 8:27–35

The Bible, as we know it, is the most read book on earth. It has also been banned more than any other book. It is a bestseller that speaks of salvation and points us to eternal life, yet it is a book that people have died for and that has led to great loss of life. It is the one book that you will find in hotel rooms and prisons alike, as well as in so many homes, and yet a great many people who have access to it are largely unfamiliar with its content or message. Bibles are found in the strangest of places: in popular British imagination, every desert island has one, while at the same time Bibles for computers, laptops, tablets and phones are easily acquired. Bibles are presented at baptisms, confirmations, weddings, ordinations, the first day at school, the last day at school and numerous other occasions, although rarely at funerals, perhaps because it is too late by then. Nevertheless, a Bible may well be placed on the coffin of a Christian at their funeral. There is also the tradition of the family Bible, in which are inscribed important dates and facts about members of a family. Bibles are handed down from generation to generation, preserved for posterity and sometimes exchanged for high prices. We are surrounded by Bibles. As the apostle Paul put it to his friend Timothy, 'from childhood you have known the sacred writings that are able to instruct you for salvation through faith in Christ Jesus' (2 Timothy 3:15).

The word 'Bible' simply means 'book'. The Bible is *the* book after which every other book is named. It is the best book in the world and the paradigm of all books. There are millions and millions of copies of the Bible all over the world, in every language you can think of, and many more. It has even been translated into invented languages, such as Klingon (from *Star Trek*) and Quenya (one of the languages of the elves in Tolkien's *The Lord of the Rings*), and also into Esperanto (a constructed attempt at a global language). The Bible was written in Hebrew (the language of the Jews), Aramaic and Greek, the *lingua franca* of the first-century Middle East, and translated into Latin (the *lingua franca* of Europe) by St Jerome between 382 and 405. For many, Jerome's translation, the Vulgate, marks the birth of the Bible as we know it. It is fitting that Jerome worked on the translation while based in Bethlehem. The birth of the word-book and the birth of the Word have the same geographical location, spreading from there.

Today, copies of the Bible are present all around us. The Bible likewise imbues our spiritual lives. Church worship is steeped in the Bible; prayers and liturgies reverberate with scripture and Bible passages are read aloud in most church services. In his other letter to Timothy, Paul writes, 'give attention to the public reading of scripture, to exhorting, to teaching' (1 Timothy 4:13), and this has been a mainstay of Christian worship ever since.

Christians are, among other things, people who read the Bible – together and, in the last 500 years, alone. Since William Tyndale completed his vernacular translation of the New Testament around 1525, and Martin Luther his in 1522 (and the complete Bible in German in 1534), and with the help of printing presses developed by Gutenberg and Caxton, the Bible has become a private as well as a public book. Tyndale was reviled and eventually executed for his work, yet between 1604 and 1611 – when the compilers of the King James Version of the Bible (the Authorised Version) gathered in the Jerusalem Chamber at Westminster Abbey – Tyndale's work was purloined almost in its entirety. More than 85% of the Authorised Version's New Testament and the first half of its Old Testament plagiarise Tyndale. So today, whether we glance at a Bible gathering dust on a shelf or hold one in our hand, we are holding history – bloodstained, lethal, controversial history. Meanwhile, there are still countries today where to possess a Bible can have serious, if not deadly, consequences. The Bible is still a dangerous book.

The Bible is part of our spiritual furniture, just as it is part of the fixtures and fittings in some hotels. Remove it and our spiritual landscape, the interior decoration of our souls, would be very different, and we would soon notice its absence. I have been to humanist funerals where the officiant inadvertently quoted the Bible ('There's a time to be born and a time to die,' she said, quoting Ecclesiastes 3:2), and our language owes as much, if not more, to the King James Bible as it does to Chaucer or Shakespeare. Nevertheless, and as cautious of surveys and opinion polls as we might want to be (see 'Newspaper' next week, p. 157), a British survey conducted over

20 years ago showed that only 16% of churchgoers privately read the Bible every day, another 9% read it several times a week, 11% once a week and 9% once a month; while 18% of churchgoers said they never read the Bible at home. In 2011, a ComRes survey told us that only 8% of Britons read the Bible at all, but 46% believe it is an important book. Meanwhile, the annual research of the American Bible Society (ABS) in 2018 reported that 88% of Americans own a Bible, while 81% of them said that morals were declining in their country. The ABS categorises attitudes towards the Bible in various ways; the research showed that 17% were 'engaged', 15% 'friendly', 5% 'neutral' and 54% 'disengaged'. In the same study, 16% of those surveyed said the Bible is a daily necessity, while 19% said that social media was and 28% said they needed 'something sweet'. The biggest daily necessity of American life in 2018 was coffee, needed by 36% of respondents.

Reading figures like this, we might not only look around at our friends, acquaintances and fellow churchgoers, but also cast our minds back to the meeting between Philip and the Ethiopian. Here is someone reading the Bible privately without knowing what to make of it. He asks the question that rings loud today: 'How can I, unless someone guides me?' This is a challenge and an opportunity for us all. For those of us who read the Bible regularly and know it well, we know something that a lot of other people do not, and there are a lot of people who need to be shown what Philip showed; that is, that scripture points to one who was led to the slaughter without justice – Jesus Christ the Lord, the hero of the Bible, whose Father was the author of everything and whose Spirit lives on every page.

Trinity of love and power, we praise you for your holy word and pray always that, in regular encounter and engagement with the words of life found in the Bible, we may read, mark and inwardly digest them, washed down with reverence and humility. Amen

Monday

Piano

Three in one

> Now the eleven disciples went to Galilee, to the mountain to which Jesus had directed them. When they saw him, they worshipped him; but some doubted. And Jesus came and said to them, 'All authority in heaven and on earth has been given to me. Go therefore and make disciples of all nations, baptizing them in the name of the Father and of the Son and of the Holy Spirit, and teaching them to obey everything that I have commanded you. And remember, I am with you always, to the end of the age.'
>
> MATTHEW 28:16–20

The first pianos were made in the early 18th century by Bartolomeo Cristofori (1655–1731) and were named for their new ability to play both quietly and loudly (*piano* and *forte* in Italian; they were originally called 'fortepianos'). In this, they were an advancement on the harpsichord, which could not produce any variation in volume when played. Both instruments are composed of strings stretched horizontally in a frame, but in a harpsichord they are plucked by the key mechanism whereas in a piano they are struck by hammers, thereby introducing the possibility of hard or soft hitting, yielding loud or quiet tones. Both instruments permit the playing of more than one note at a time, allowing the playing of chords rather than single sounds – harmony rather than melody alone.

A piano is a wonder of technology, an object of high craftsmanship and a producer of beautiful sounds. Before the relatively recent advent of electronic keyboards, it was common to see one in a home, even if no one could play it adequately. It is evident from the novels of Jane Austen, though, that young women were expected to be able to play the piano to a decent standard and to accompany singers, so that a common form of entertainment, the parlour recital, could be offered for guests in an age not yet provided with the copious alternative options we now have. The piano may have had its heyday, but today's models are better made than they have ever been, and a handmade Steinway or Bechstein is a prized possession. Meanwhile, old, decrepit instruments are almost worthless, and removing one to the scrap heap can be expensive.

Whether a piano is a prized grand, a beat-up upright or an electronic keyboard or organ, it can do the same thing: it can produce a chord (as can a guitar or harp). A basic chord is made of three notes: the tonic (keynote), the third (mediant) and the fifth note (dominant) of the scale. In C major, these are C, E and G. If the chord is minor rather than major, the middle note is flattened (to E flat), which gives a more melancholy flavour to the whole.

Most western music is built on chords, such that even a simple tune has a harmonic foundation, that is, it can be accompanied by chords. Hymn tunes exemplify this idea of a melody with chords 'underneath', and the choir can sing these notes as well, creating a rich sound. There are 'rules' of harmony, although, as with many of the arts, the breaking of these rules epitomises the 20th century!

The harmony of a chord made up of three notes provides a remarkable metaphor for helping us to contemplate what it might be for our God to be Trinity. The creed attributed to St Athanasius (298–373) describes the doctrine of the Trinity:

> There is one Father, not three Fathers; one Son, not three Sons; one Holy Ghost, not three Holy Ghosts. And in this Trinity none is before, or after another; none is greater, or less than another. But the whole three Persons are co-eternal and co-equal.

The doctrine of the Holy Trinity, which characterises the Christian faith and makes it unique, is the mystery through which we understand God as a being of relationship manifested in the inseparability of the Father-creator, the Son-Christ and the Holy Spirit, ever-present among us. We have different names for these, and we hold that God is all three and all three are one God.

If you play a note on the piano, you hear a single sound (although that sound is made up of a blend of overtones, as other strings vibrate in sympathy). Playing a second note introduces a relationship between the two notes, such that if one is altered the relationship changes; it sounds different. Playing a C with a G does not sound the same as playing a C with an F. Add a third note, and the sound changes again and there is a three-way relationship. The ensuing chord is one, made of three notes in relationship. In C major, usually the C is on the bottom, then the E and then the G, in a major triad. But it can be reversed, such that the G or the E can be the bass note. It may sound slightly different, but it employs the same noises and is the same chord, in either root position or first or second inversions. Spread the notes out and you have a 'broken' chord or *arpeggio*. Master the theory and performance of this basic concept and you will be well on the way to being something of a composer or pianist!

This musical metaphor is not a perfect one for explaining the Trinitarian nature of God, but it may be helpful. A triad is three notes in one, a sound made up of three sounds, which can be heard separately, but which make up something that is greater than the sum of their parts when put together. The musical universe as we know it is built upon this foundation. However, as Athanasius found when trying to describe God, there comes a point when we must stop and accept our inability to do so fully with words. Sixteen hundred years after Athanasius, the philosopher Ludwig Wittgenstein (1889–1951) wrote a similar thing in his *Tractatus Logico-Philosophicus*: 'What we cannot speak about we must pass over in silence.'

Or rather, we might turn to music to take us just a little further, beyond the realm of words. If you have a piano in your house, then it may yet provide a stepping stone to a slightly deeper comprehension of the mystery that is God – Father, Son and Holy Spirit. Play a triad chord on it and, listening to the blend of three-in-one, contemplate the mystery of God, our creator, our redeemer and the sustainer of faith and life.

God, you are the root of the universe, and have turned your world upside down by sending your Son to resolve the sin of the world. By your Spirit, may we find our lives and desires always in harmony with your will. Amen

Tuesday

Night light

Floundering in the dark

Now there was a Pharisee named Nicodemus, a leader of the Jews. He came to Jesus by night and said to him, 'Rabbi, we know that you are a teacher who has come from God; for no one can do these signs that you do apart from the presence of God.' Jesus answered him, 'Very truly, I tell you, no one can see the kingdom of God without being born from above... And this is the judgement, that the light has come into the world, and people loved darkness rather than light because their deeds were evil. For all who do evil hate the light and do not come to the light, so that their deeds may not be exposed. But those who do what is true come to the light, so that it may be clearly seen that their deeds have been done in God.'

JOHN 3:1–3, 19–21

Do you have any of those night lights that come on automatically when you walk past them, or are perhaps on all the time, glowing gently to illuminate nocturnal trips to the bathroom or to the fridge for a midnight snack? Sometimes children have them in their bedrooms, so that the room is never completely dark, which for some is frightening. It is rare to experience total darkness, the kind where you are completely blind – you cannot see your hand in front of your face and if you try to move you will bump into things or fall over and perhaps do yourself some damage. This is why at home, if you do get up in the middle of the night, a night light gently glowing in the hallway can be not only reassuring but also downright helpful. It is the same technology that people have in their driveways and by the door to illuminate visitors in the dark. We like to light up our darkness, so we can know what is going on, be reassured and feel confident and safe that no one is up to no good under the cloak of night. In the light, human beings feel safe; in the dark, we feel disoriented, uneasy, even fearful.

When we think of Nicodemus, the Pharisee, a leader of the Jewish people, coming to Jesus by night, a little night light bulb switches on in our minds: why would he do that? The obvious answer is that he wants to use the darkness as cover; he does not want to be seen. Because of who he is, he cannot be seen to seek out Jesus for a theological discussion, yet that is exactly what he wants. Ironically, to have such a conversation safely and openly, Nicodemus must do it at night, in the dark: secretly, clandestinely, even dangerously. To modern humans, who are still active at night, the strangeness of this scenario is weakened, as we take for granted the light bulbs, timer switches and constant electricity supply that make sunset simply a moment in the day that we sometimes do not even notice. In Jesus' time, people got up at dawn, and once the sun had set the day was deemed to be over. Staying up past sunset required oil lamps to be lit, which were slightly dangerous, short-lived and, inevitably, costly. So for Nicodemus to approach Jesus by night would have been a brave, maverick thing for him to do, and it would have taken Jesus by surprise, unless of course the meeting was prearranged.

Whether or not Jesus was expecting Nicodemus' visit, their conversation gets to the heart of what was to become the Christian faith. It also affects Nicodemus deeply, for he reappears in John 7:50–51, asking for a fair trial for Jesus. More significantly, he is described as assisting Joseph of Arimathea in giving Jesus a decent burial (John 19:39). In that story, Nicodemus is acting neither alone nor at night, for it is important that the burial of Jesus be done before nightfall. Between this story of Nicodemus visiting Jesus by night and his reappearance as a disciple, Nicodemus has moved from the darkness of night into the light of day. He does this both literally and metaphorically as his spiritual journey with Christ unfolds.

In this respect, Nicodemus is both special and ordinary. He is special because he is a leader, a government man, a member of the hierarchy out of whose line he should not step. Yet he is also Everyman, in that he is someone seeking knowledge and wanting to find out about and discuss the new views that are the talk of the town.

We are all in the dark when it comes to faith. Only Christ can illuminate our faith, for he is the light of the world. As we flounder about, like Nicodemus, feeling our way in the unlit world, we live in hope that sometimes a night light will come on and show us the way to go. Sure enough, these lights do come on at various points, although if we have our eyes closed we fail to notice. Sadly, so many people do not recognise the glimmers of light in the world that have the potential to burst into a blaze of light to illuminate our path. When news bulletins are so bleak, when we are culturally conditioned to be cynical, or when we have bought into the ludicrous claim that science and religion are in opposition, we find that understanding cannot grow from faith, because what little faith there is never sees any light, being locked away in the darkness of our contemporary, passing age.

Yet those lights do come on even in the night-times of our souls. They may flicker dimly amid the gloom of sin, despair or complacency, but they are there. Christ's light is always there, ready to burst upon us in response to a little faith, a little hope and a little love. May the night lights in your home be a gentle, comforting, guiding reminder of that eternal promise of light, brought into the world by Jesus Christ, the Word incarnate and hope of the world.

Jesus, our glowing Lord, grant your light always to illuminate our path, so that whatever state our faith is in, our flickering love may be ready to respond to your call to follow, and so burgeon into the light of understanding and truth. Amen

Wednesday

Curtains

Behind the veil

> When it was noon, darkness came over the whole land until three in the afternoon. At three o'clock Jesus cried out with a loud voice, 'Eloi, Eloi, lema sabachthani?' which means, 'My God, my God, why have you forsaken me?' When some of the bystanders heard it, they said, 'Listen, he is calling for Elijah.' And someone ran, filled a sponge with sour wine, put it on a stick, and gave it to him to drink, saying, 'Wait, let us see whether Elijah will come to take him down.' Then Jesus gave a loud cry and breathed his last. And the curtain of the temple was torn in two, from top to bottom. Now when the centurion, who stood facing him, saw that in this way he breathed his last, he said, 'Truly this man was God's Son!'
>
> MARK 15:33–39

In the book of Exodus, we find some of the earliest instructions for making and hanging curtains. When Moses relates God's instructions for building the tabernacle (Exodus 26) he specifies that there should be 'ten curtains of fine twisted linen, and blue, purple, and crimson yarns' (Exodus 26:1); that each curtain should be 28 cubits long and 4 cubits wide (42 feet by 6 feet); and that the curtains should be joined together with blue loops and gold and brass clasps, making two sets of five. Another special curtain was made to separate 'the most holy place'. This curtain was to have cherubim embroidered on it and attached to 'four pillars of acacia overlaid with gold, which have hooks of gold and rest on four bases of silver' (Exodus 26:32). These curtains, which must have been a splendid sight, were for concealment, to hide the most holy place from prying, unworthy eyes. Only once a year did anyone pass through them to minister in the most sacred place, as Zechariah did before the birth of John the Baptist (Luke 1:8). Curtains confer privacy and, whether we are trying to stop strangers peering into our houses or protecting a holy place, the principle and practice is the same.

It is perhaps strange, therefore, that the domestic use of curtains is not so ancient. The use of curtains to protect domestic privacy seems to have been introduced around the mid-17th century in Holland, where curtains that covered only the bottom half of downstairs windows – suggesting their primary purpose was not to block out light – started to appear. Even so, it took a while for this custom to be adopted; most Dutch houses did not have curtains at all because faithful (Calvinist) Christians had nothing to hide! Nevertheless, in the UK at least, the idea of the inside of our homes being visible from the street is unpalatable, leading to the development of net curtains, which let in light but obscure vision. The fact that it was in busy London that the popularity for curtains grew in the 18th century also suggests that privacy was the motivating factor.

By the mid-19th century, curtains had become ubiquitous, and their ability to shut out light was increasingly valued alongside the arrival of gas and then electric lighting. Furthermore, we find the recurrence of the idea of separation: just as the curtain of the temple in Jerusalem separated the most holy place, the well-curtained home could also be considered as 'separated' from the rest of the world. In the last couple of hundred years, especially in the UK, the home has become a sanctuary, protected and concealed by curtains. Whatever goes on at home does so behind closed doors and curtains.

We might remember this as we open our curtains in the morning and draw them close at night. In the morning, light floods in when we open the curtains, and that itself is a powerful daily moment, but it is only possible if we have denied the dawn and kept the light out. Curtains both protect privacy and control the light. Spiritually speaking, however, we can do neither. For the Lord knows the inner secrets of our hearts (Psalm 44:21), and we cannot hide from God (Psalm 139:7). In the temple the presence of God was hidden, concealed behind a curtain, inaccessible to humanity, but the psalmist reminds us that, while humans could not see through the curtain, it did not stop God seeing into our souls. This curtain being torn in half at the moment of Christ's death is therefore deeply significant, because it heralds a completely different understanding of the relationship between God and humanity, a real separation between the old and the new covenants; the division of the temple curtain (sometimes called the 'veil') marks the transition from Old to New Testament. In Jesus Christ, God is not hidden, but revealed in human form for all to see. Raised on the cross, the earthly life of Christ comes to a very public end, such that his incarnational self-sacrifice itself represents the opening of that curtain. As the writer of Hebrews puts it, 'we have confidence to enter the sanctuary by the blood of Jesus, by the new and living way that he opened for us through the curtain (that is, through his flesh)' (Hebrews 10:19–20). After the resurrection, Jesus goes on to reveal himself as risen Saviour to 'more than five hundred' people (1 Corinthians 15:6), and is revealed in the life and mission of the church, through the Holy Spirit, to this very day.

The idea that God has revealed himself to the world through the saving work and person of Christ is one of the most profound and mind-boggling truths of the Christian faith, indeed of any faith. It is what makes Christianity so unique and powerful, combining in the physical being of Jesus the essence of both divinity and humanity, and showing how, uniquely, they can be combined once for all and forever in 'Jesus Christ, the Son of God' (Mark 1:1). This is perhaps something we pass over in our daily life and faith, forgetting the scale of what God has done in Christ. Meanwhile, twice a day we draw our curtains, and in doing so might recall the light of the world, that is, Jesus, flooding in, removing the curtain of concealment that, in the era before Christ, denied all but very few access to the throne of grace.

Jesus, part the curtains of our souls and look with mercy upon our wrongdoings and infirmities. For by your cross and resurrection, you have removed the barrier of sin, revealed yourself and set us free. Amen

Thursday

Salt shaker

The flavour of faith

> When Jesus saw the crowds, he went up the mountain; and after he sat down, his disciples came to him. Then he began to speak, and taught them, saying:
>
> 'Blessed are the poor in spirit, for theirs is the kingdom of heaven.
>
> 'Blessed are those who mourn, for they will be comforted.
>
> 'Blessed are the meek, for they will inherit the earth.
>
> 'Blessed are those who hunger and thirst for righteousness, for they will be filled.
>
> 'Blessed are the merciful, for they will receive mercy.
>
> 'Blessed are the pure in heart, for they will see God.
>
> 'Blessed are the peacemakers, for they will be called children of God.
>
> 'Blessed are those who are persecuted for righteousness' sake, for theirs is the kingdom of heaven.
>
> 'Blessed are you when people revile you and persecute you and utter all kinds of evil against you falsely on my account. Rejoice and be glad, for your reward is great in heaven, for in the same way they persecuted the prophets who were before you.
>
> 'You are the salt of the earth; but if salt has lost its taste, how can its saltiness be restored? It is no longer good for anything, but is thrown out and trampled under foot.'
>
> MATTHEW 5:1–13

I do not like the taste of salt very much. Too much salt is bad for you, and many people add it to almost everything they eat. In my opinion, this just makes the food taste of salt, but I accept that for many people salt enhances the flavour. Others add it to the water in which they cook vegetables or pasta, and salt is used to cure meat and fish and to make bread and cheese. Even if you never add salt to your meals, there is still plenty of it present in what we eat, as so much food needs a least a pinch of it. Like it or not, salt is ubiquitous.

Salt is composed of sodium and chloride. If you pour hydrochloric acid on your hand, it will take less than a minute to burn it away. Drink it and you will die horribly and very quickly. But if you add sodium to hydrochloride you get salt, which is one of the most commonly useful substances we know. Indeed, without it we could not survive. This partly explains why salt was so costly in Jesus' time. It was so valuable as a preservative that it was often traded ounce-for-ounce with gold. Roman soldiers were paid in salt, which is how we get the word *salary*. If a Roman soldier didn't do his job, he wouldn't get all of his salt – or, as the turn of phrase still puts it, he wasn't 'worth his salt'.

Salt relates to value and preservation, then and now. Jesus uses it as a metaphor. Think of our world now, and consider how much worse things would be if there was no Christianity and no churches. By churches, of course, I mean the people who gather in the buildings, not the buildings themselves! Churches contain good-hearted, straightforward, loving, faithful folk, like you and me, striving to make a difference in whatever way they can. Such people try to live and preach the gospel of salvation and model in their lives the love of God for all people. In this sense, we are and need to be salty: valuable, preservative people.

But we should be careful. As Jesus goes on to say, 'If salt has lost its taste, how can its saltiness be restored?' (v. 13). This relates to the Dead Sea, which is more than a mile-and-a-half below sea level, and from which much of the salt that was used in Palestine came. The Dead Sea has an inlet from the river Jordan but no outlet. The hot sun evaporates the water and leaves behind a chunky white powder made up of a combination of salt and minerals. This salt, therefore, is not pure sodium chloride, so if the air gets a bit damp the salt dissolves and dissipates. If that happens, the salt loses its seasoning, as Jesus puts it – a phenomenon that his hearers would have understood and tried to avoid. For then, as Jesus goes on to say, 'It is no longer good for anything, but is thrown out and trampled under foot' (v. 13) – it becomes literally 'good for nothing'. It cannot be thrown into a garden or field, because it would taint the soil and kill anything that was planted. Instead, it would be thrown on to the roads where it would gradually be ground into the dirt and disappear, ultimately to be walked over. Such salt has not served its purpose, and indeed has been allowed to decay; it has been damaged by air and water and become useless.

The same happens to the salt in our cupboards today. If you leave salt in the shaker and do not use it, grinding it or shaking it out into the world (on to your food), then it gets damp in the pot, solidifies perhaps, and is basically no good. Salt does not have a use-by date as such, but it must be kept under the right conditions, just as it needed to be in Jesus' time. Salt that is not looked after becomes useless.

Some people say that the greatest threat to Christianity is not communism, atheism, materialism or humanism. Rather, the greatest threat to Christianity are Christians who try to sneak into heaven incognito without ever sharing their faith, without ever living out the Christian life, without ever becoming involved in the most significant work God is doing on earth. This is exactly what Jesus was talking about in the part of the sermon on the mount from which we get this little passage about salt. The gathered crowd to whom Jesus was speaking was not the United Nations General Assembly nor Parliament, but rather a group of common people living ordinary lives, meeting on a hillside. They were under occupation; they couldn't make their own laws; they couldn't plan their own futures; so Jesus gives them words of hope and encouragement known as the beatitudes, and then tells them that they 'are the salt of the earth… the light of the world' (vv. 13–14). It was certainly a radical and bemusing thing to say or hear.

Yet, now as then, we all know what salt is; we all have salt, even if in the 21st century we pay so much less for it. Next time you sprinkle salt in the pan or on your meal, remember that as disciples of Jesus, in every age, we are blessed in so many ways, and that it is also our calling to be a blessing to others. Like salt, we are called to season the world, to bring out the fulsome flavour of faith, so that all may taste and see how gracious the Lord is.

Jesus, help us be salt to a world made bland by self-interest and ignorance, not decaying in reticence, but shaken out to season your people with faith, hope and love. Amen

Friday

Dining table

The Lord's table

> When they came to the place that God had shown him, Abraham built an altar there and laid the wood in order. He bound his son Isaac, and laid him on the altar, on top of the wood. Then Abraham reached out his hand and took the knife to kill his son. But the angel of the Lord called to him from heaven, and said, 'Abraham, Abraham!' And he said, 'Here I am.' He said, 'Do not lay your hand on the boy or do anything to him; for now I know that you fear God, since you have not withheld your son, your only son, from me.' And Abraham looked up and saw a ram, caught in a thicket by its horns. Abraham went and took the ram and offered it up as a burnt-offering instead of his son. So Abraham called that place 'The Lord will provide'; as it is said to this day, 'On the mount of the Lord it shall be provided.'
>
> GENESIS 22:9–14

Most churches have a table. Usually placed at the back of the hall, it has leaflets, hymn books, service sheets, mislaid spectacles, collection plates and other parish paraphernalia on it. There is likely to be another table at the other end of the church too: this table could well have nothing on it at all, or it might have a fair linen cloth on it, and perhaps candles, a book stand, a cross and a Bible. Between these two tables – one functional, the other liturgical – are the pews, the seats for the people. On a Sunday morning, we place ourselves in that space between the practicalities of daily life and the celebration of eternal life.

The altar table – as many, but not all, would call it – has a long history, stretching back to pre-Christian, Jewish and pagan times. It was a place of sacrifice, where an animal or human was ceremoniously murdered as an offering to the gods. The sacrifice of living creatures on an altar may be seen as an offering of food to the gods; the sacrificial lamb or goat was dinner for the deity, even though ultimately the poor creature was devoured in flame or otherwise eaten by the priests. The failure of a sacrifice to produce rain, grant victory in battle or cure a disease was taken as a sign that the sacrifice was insufficient or unworthy, such that often many more sacrifices were made to appease or appeal to the gods. There was a connection to sin too; the sacrifice was also an atonement, a making-up for the bad things that had been done. As well as seeking good things, the altar was also a place where forgiveness for bad things was sought.

Such demands apparently made by the gods were unbearable, especially where parents were required to offer up their children, as Abraham was. He builds an altar, a divine dinner table, and in a macabre twist Isaac helps him. It is reminiscent of all those wartime victims who were forced to dig their own graves before being shot. For Abraham and Isaac, notwithstanding how awful it must have felt, it is but a test, which quietly reveals a cultural background in which the idea was not unthinkable. One of the main messages of God's releasing Abraham from going through with the sacrifice is to help the Israelites understand that whatever their rivals may do and think, their (one) God does not demand human sacrifice.

For Christians, this story resonates loudly with Christ's sacrifice, the paschal lamb who by his own blood redeemed the world. Just as God spares Isaac and tells Abraham to grab a nearby sheep, he does the same when it comes to Christ: rather than call for the death of all his children, his one Son, Jesus, is substituted on the cross, an atoning sacrifice who bears the sins of the world as Messiah, the Christ.

There is, however, a twist here: the death of Christ is not the end. For in no other sacrifice, before or since, has the victim lived again, defeating the power of death and rising again. Just as Christ dies for all, he also rises for all, defeating the logic of punishment for sin, removing the need for any request to be accompanied by sacrifice and rewriting the spiritual future of humanity. In this we hold Christ to be, rolled into one, the victim, the saviour and, as the one who offers himself as the sacrifice, the priest who presides over the self-offering made on the altar of the cross. Thus, Christ is both priest and victim: 'He has appeared once for all at the end of the age to remove sin by the sacrifice of himself' (Hebrews 9:26).

At this time of year in particular, but also on any day when the Eucharist is celebrated, we remember how Christ flagged up his status as 'the lamb of God who takes away the sin of the world', as John the Baptist put it (John 1:29). The key event is the last supper, at which, around Passover time, Jesus presided over a Passover meal, recasting it as a pointer to his death and resurrection. The first Passover (Exodus 12) was a quick meal, where lambs or goats were swiftly dispatched to provide fast food for a long journey of rescue. At the last supper, Christ tells his disciples that it is he himself whom they are eating and drinking, and commands them to 'do this in remembrance of me' (Luke 22:19). Thus, he connects himself not only to the Passover (paschal) lamb, but also to Moses, the one who led his people to freedom from slavery, which in our case is the slavery to sin. Jesus is not only the paschal lamb but also the second exodus.

Jesus did not celebrate that Passover meal at an altar or table, as the Greco-Roman Jewish custom was to recline on couches to eat. The reason we have altar tables in churches relates more to the tradition of a place where religious offerings are made than to any idea of a dinner table around which the disciples sat. Yet we have come to use the phrase 'the Lord's table' as the place at which we commemorate and celebrate anew that 'meal' (mass) that Jesus ate with his friends and followers.

The Lord's table at which we celebrate the Eucharist is therefore both an ordinary table and a special table. It is a table of communion, and on it we rest our collective memory of all that Christ did. It is the table of companionship in Christ, where we eat bread together (which is what 'companionship' literally means). This is also what our dining table at home is for: it is for companionship, for not only eating at, but also sharing company (a word related to 'companion'), fellowship, conversation, discussion and debate. The dining table is a place of relationship among human beings; the altar table is the place where the relationship between humanity and God is remembered and renewed in the recollection of the redemption and resurrection wrought by God in Jesus Christ.

Every table is the Lord's table. We meet Christ around every table, and there is an altar in every house. As is written on an anonymous inscription some people have at home, 'God is the head of this house, the unseen guest at every meal, the silent listener at every conversation.' Unworthy as we are, may there always be a place at our tables for Christ.

Lord Jesus, be the unseen but welcome guest at our tables, even when we eat alone, so that, nourished by you, we may welcome others in your name. Amen

Saturday

Chair

Are you sitting comfortably?

> As Jesus was walking along, he saw a man called Matthew
> sitting at the tax booth; and he said to him, 'Follow me.' And
> he got up and followed him.
>
> And as he sat at dinner in the house, many tax-collectors
> and sinners came and were sitting with him and his disciples.
> When the Pharisees saw this, they said to his disciples, 'Why
> does your teacher eat with tax-collectors and sinners?' But
> when he heard this, he said, 'Those who are well have no
> need of a physician, but those who are sick. Go and learn
> what this means, "I desire mercy, not sacrifice." For I have
> come to call not the righteous but sinners.'
>
> MATTHEW 9:9–13

Most of us try to sit comfortably when watching TV, talking to friends
or eating a meal. We sit at the theatre, at concerts and in church. In
church, we tend to sit for the readings, the sermon and performances
by the choir or music group. When we have received Communion,
we will often sit and wait quietly while others go up to the rail. We
might sit, or we might kneel, for the prayers. In a more formal choral
evensong service, we sit for the psalm, readings and anthem, but
stand for the Magnificat and Nunc Dimittis, and we are expected to
kneel for the prayers.

We spend between a quarter and a third of our day asleep, probably
lying down (see 'Bed', p. 180), and another significant proportion
of our day sitting, depending on our job or lifestyle. Some smart
watches include a feature, which cannot be switched off, that gives

the wearer a little tap on the wrist if they have not stood up in the last hour. Remaining seated for more than an hour at a time is considered to be unhealthy, and we should stand up and walk about for five minutes each hour, the technology giants tell us. Going to church, with all that standing, sitting and kneeling, is clearly very healthy!

Prayer is generally associated with kneeling: a posture of supplication and humility, although this can be a difficult, even painful posture for some. Singing is invariably done standing up, for good reason, as it involves the inhalation and expulsion of air from the diaphragm, which is easier and more comfortable, powerful and effective when standing. In the medieval period, there were no chairs in churches; folk milled about, came and went, perhaps to catch the music, which largely went on while the priest celebrated Communion almost out of sight. The architecture of medieval churches therefore made no provision for pews or chairs; at best, there were stone benches set into the outer walls, which only those who could not stand used, and thus it was said that 'the weakest went to the wall'. This began to change during the Reformation, as it brought with it an increased emphasis on the word, rather than the sacrament, which in turn made the sermon more important. Benches began to appear, and it became increasingly necessary to sit near the front in order to hear the sermon, and the position of one's pew was determined by social standing and wealth. Pew rents were introduced, a practice that has not completely died out. Many a village church has box pews with a slot on the door for the name card of the 'owner', and woe betide the newcomer or visitor who sits in the wrong pew!

At home, there are different ways to 'take a pew'. Dining chairs, armchairs, sofas and desk chairs are for different sedentary activities, and nowadays manufacturers are concerned with our posture as well as our comfort. In the past, sitting was not such a common activity and, during the Middle Ages, chairs were rare in homes. Chairs denoted power and status. At Louis XIV's court, rank was indicated by what you sat on: first a chair with arms, then one with a back, then a stool with a back, then an ordinary stool and, for the lower ranked, a folding stool. Some people did not get to sit down at all but had to remain standing. Upholstery was developed at the end of the 17th century, adding a further layer of comfort.

It is still customary to stand in the presence of someone senior and for differences in rank or authority to be expressed in terms of who sits and who stands, whether a king seated on a throne (see Isaiah 6:1 and Revelation 4) or an errant child standing before the desk behind which the teacher is seated. Since it is polite to stand up when someone enters the room, not to do so either displays rudeness or tacitly claims authority.

When Jesus sees him collecting taxes, Matthew is sitting at his booth. He is probably sitting on some kind of bench, waiting for people to come and pay him, as surely they must. It is a posture not so much of relaxation or even work, but of authority, resented as it was by most people. Tax collectors had power, which they notoriously abused, taking more than they should, as the short, tree-climbing Zacchaeus did (Luke 19:1–10). Jesus then goes to Matthew's house, where they sit down to eat together. They would not have sat on the kind of chairs we use today, though, for the diners would recline, and typically there were three people on each of three couches. The most important people would recline on the central couch, often with one of them presiding over ('chairing') the discussion. In this case, it is Jesus; he goes there not just to eat but to teach. The Pharisees do not like it: they think that, as a man of God, Jesus should not go near such impromptu dinner discussions. Because he does so, they ultimately and logically conclude that he is not properly a man of God at all and turn against him. Nevertheless, Jesus sat down with sinners and tax collectors on their territory and made it his own.

We sit down in various contexts and situations, giving it no thought. We like comfort and demand it of our chairs. As we sit in our comfortably upholstered chair or at a desk or dining table, let us think of Jesus' call to Matthew as being like a little tap on the wrist from Jesus, telling us, 'Get up and follow me.' For the Lord knows our rising up and our sitting down, our going out and coming in (Isaiah 37:28).

Jesus, let us not sit in sin, but rise to your call to follow and make disciples of your people, so that whether we stand or sit, we may do so always to your honour and glory. Amen

Palm Sunday

Newspaper

Public opinion

The disciples went and did as Jesus had directed them; they brought the donkey and the colt, and put their cloaks on them, and he sat on them. A very large crowd spread their cloaks on the road, and others cut branches from the trees and spread them on the road. The crowds that went ahead of him and that followed were shouting,

'Hosanna to the Son of David!
Blessed is the one who comes in the name of the Lord!
Hosanna in the highest heaven!'

When he entered Jerusalem, the whole city was in turmoil, asking, 'Who is this?' The crowds were saying, 'This is the prophet Jesus from Nazareth in Galilee.'

MATTHEW 21:6–11

In Broxbourne, Hertfordshire, is the printing plant that produces several of our major newspapers daily. Every 20 minutes a lorry arrives with huge rolls of paper from Scandinavia, and these are automatically loaded on to a conveyor system that logs, moves and delivers them to the printing presses with timely accuracy and efficiency. The printing of a newspaper is a technologically advanced operation. The paper travels through the presses at about 30mph, and at that speed if the paper tears or breaks, hundreds of copies are wasted. From imaging on a computer screen to folding and stapling, the production of a newspaper is a single, uninterrupted process. At the end of the line are pallets waiting to be put on to lorries, which within minutes can join the nearby motorway to deliver the papers nationwide, bearing news, stories, criticism, gossip, information, opinion polls and perhaps even 'fake news'. The sheer mass of this media is breathtaking.

Since World War II, interest and expertise in measuring public opinion has grown. Ipsos MORI has dominated the world of opinion polls, producing carefully sourced and balanced market research data to be mulled over by newspapers and broadcasters. They have sometimes been accused of 'getting it wrong', especially in the wake of the 2015 and 2017 UK general elections, but nevertheless the predictions of the market researchers are usually fairly accurate. We must, however, always be careful to distinguish between opinion and fact.

When Jesus entered Jerusalem on a donkey, the crowd knew who he was (or they thought they did). The media of the time (grapevine and gossip) had the whole city in turmoil, wondering who he was, but Matthew also tells us that some of the crowd knew, and the buzz got around that this was Jesus, the prophet from Nazareth. The word spread fast. Nowadays, when the media are pushing headlines to our screens even while a story is unfolding, and newspapers are rushing to get something coherent on to tomorrow's front page, we can play with the idea of what the media would have said about the arrival of Jesus into Jerusalem on what we now call Palm Sunday. Various Easter TV programmes and books have done this over the years with mixed results. We can contemplate what it might have been like to be in the crowd, to hear the questions and answers fly to and fro, to see this strange figure apparently fulfilling prophecy and to join in the ancient acclamation from the Psalms. 'Hosanna' means 'Save us', and is found in Psalm 118:25: 'Save us, we beseech you, O Lord! O Lord, we beseech you, give us success!'

Public opinion was *for* Jesus that day. Public opinion was that he was a good thing, a Saviour who could deliver them from whatever it was that they wanted to be delivered from. Freedom from Rome, oppression, religious repression, poverty, taxation, hunger, bullying, injustice: all or any of these things could have been in the minds of those shouting 'Hosanna!' Sadly, it seems none of them really knew who Jesus was or what he was offering. We can never know, because there were no pollsters or market researchers on hand to ask them, so no data to be interpreted or manipulated. We do have Matthew, though, whose description we take to be accurate.

Similarly, only four days later, another crowd gathered to hear Pontius Pilate ask what to do with the same man, and, undoubtedly stirred up, this self-selecting sample of public opinion called for his death. There was no survey, no voting, no democracy involved at all. A mob both hailed Jesus and endorsed his execution. Pilate had asked Jesus, 'What is truth?' (John 18:38), and then went on to bow to the Latin adage *vox populi, vox dei* ('the voice of the people is the voice of God').

Today, the echoes of this incoherent and dangerous manifestation of public opinion is as chilling as it was for Jesus and his close friends, as our society seems to be increasingly defined by the same idea. The public did not *know* who he was, so they *decided* who he was. Then, four days later, they changed their minds and decided he was something else. As in our age today, what they decided depended on what they were told, and what they were told was either only partially true or downright false. So it came to pass that public opinion hailed Christ as conquering king and, within a week, put him on the cross.

In a lecture at the University of Kent on 25 January 2013, Sir Robert Worcester, who founded MORI in 1969, said:

Opinions: the ripples on the surface of the public's consciousness, shallow and easily changed; attitudes: the currents below the surface, deeper and stronger; and values: the deep tides of public mood, slow to change, but powerful.

On Palm Sunday, it was clearly *opinion* that shouted 'Hosanna!' But that opinion reflected *attitudes* of hatred towards Rome and the other injustices the people were experiencing. What were the *values* of the first-century Jerusalem mob? Whatever they were, they were drowned by self-interest, desperation or perhaps both. Self-interest and desperation might explain their apparent fickleness and connect them to so many of the crowds who gather in squares all over the world today as hopeful revolutions give way, as they usually do, to tyranny and oppression.

It was the equivalent of the Jerusalem media that altered public opinion and made a fool of the people, first acclaiming and then condemning Jesus. But before we blame anyone, remember that the public was the crowd: a self-selecting sample of floating voters who listened to whoever shouted the loudest. There were many who were not in the crowd on either occasion, whose measured opinions, attitudes and values were never heard that day. Next time you pick up a newspaper and scan its facts and opinions, consider where the opinions it helps you form might lead.

Jesus, you were both hailed and harrowed by unthinking, uninformed and desperate opinion. Build in us truly Christian values that in our attitudes and opinions we may always be true to you. Amen

Holy Monday

Bills

Render to God

> Then the Pharisees went and plotted to entrap him in what
> he said. So they sent their disciples to him, along with the
> Herodians, saying, 'Teacher, we know that you are sincere,
> and teach the way of God in accordance with truth, and
> show deference to no one; for you do not regard people
> with partiality. Tell us, then, what you think. Is it lawful
> to pay taxes to the emperor, or not?' But Jesus, aware of
> their malice, said, 'Why are you putting me to the test, you
> hypocrites? Show me the coin used for the tax.' And they
> brought him a denarius. Then he said to them, 'Whose head is
> this, and whose title?' They answered, 'The emperor's.' Then
> he said to them, 'Give therefore to the emperor the things
> that are the emperor's, and to God the things that are God's.'
> When they heard this, they were amazed; and they left him
> and went away.
>
> MATTHEW 22:15–22

When Jesus is asked, 'Should we pay tax to the emperor or not?', the
key word is 'or'. It is a closed question, restricting Jesus to an either/
or answer. It is also a trick question, because to answer 'No' would
be rebellious against Rome, and to say 'Yes' would be tantamount
to blasphemy. Jesus is not drawn, though, nor forced to take sides,
but tells the Pharisees' disciples to render to Caesar what is Caesar's
and to God what is God's. The attempt to confine him to an either/
or mentality fails, as Jesus sidesteps it and asks them an awkward
question, to which they must give a closed answer: 'Whose head is
this?... The emperor's (vv. 20–21).

Jesus uses a technique made famous by the Greek philosopher Socrates. The Socratic method was immortalised by Plato, who in recording the philosopher's deeds and sayings showed us a master of the method of question-and-answer teaching. This famous account of Jesus catching out the Pharisees reveals how it is possible to mentally manoeuvre an opponent into a corner by understanding and then exposing their hidden preconceptions. The Pharisees' disciples approach Jesus with the Herodians – supporters of the Roman puppet King Herod – and they are actually asking him whose side he is on. The Pharisees pretend to support Roman rule in order to cause trouble, and this is why Jesus accuses them of hypocrisy. So to support Roman taxation was to support the Roman occupation of Judea, but to object was to support insurrection. It was an awkward question, putting Jesus in a tight spot.

Jesus' ultimate answer, 'Give therefore to the emperor the things that are the emperor's, and to God the things that are God's' (v. 21), is a both/and answer to the either/or question. Jesus' interlocutors don't like a blurred answer like this, but nowadays we live by such fuzziness. In a sense, Jesus gives a 21st-century answer to a first-century question. Jesus' general response to being asked an awkward question is to ask an awkward question in return. We might remember that Jesus does a similar thing when the woman caught in adultery is brought before him (John 8:1–11). He says to the scribes and Pharisees, 'Let anyone among you who is without sin be the first to throw a stone at her.' They all slink away.

In these situations, Jesus is effectively saying, 'Think differently. See it another way. Don't squeeze things into your box that isn't my box.' For God's ways are not our ways. The kind of kingdom to which Christ points us is different: different rules, and a different logic, apply. This way of thinking was strange to the closed-minded Pharisees. Jesus' logic is not that of the Jewish law, which basically said, 'Do this, that and the other and you will be saved'. Rather, Christ's logic comes from the basic fact that God is our creator, redeemer and sustainer who no longer operates from a position of law but of loving mercy. In that logic, there is no need to see the emperor as an enemy to hate, nor even as the opposite, a friend. In Christ, even enemies are to be loved (see Matthew 5:44).

The emperor is who he is, and God is who he is. The emperor is the one in charge and taxes are due to him because taxes are payable to the ruling authorities. It was ever thus and remains so. But God is *God*, and Jesus is effectively implying that the Pharisees do not actually know what that means. It does not simply mean that God is the one who sets the laws, punishes transgressors and demands resistance to earthly powers. Rather, it means that God is – well, *God*; no more, no less. *God* is God – not the emperor, whose head is on the coin and who was considered by some to be a god. On one level, the question Jesus is asked is, 'Which of these is God: the emperor or God?' It is not linguistically possible for anyone or anything other than God to be God. *God* is God, and God is *God*.

The paying of taxes is a side issue. Pay taxes, by all means, Jesus says. It is a good idea and saves a lot of hassle if one does. The same can be said for other bills, invoices and debts. But we should make sure that we also give to God the praise and honour due to his name. So it may be that a tax or gas bill can be a reminder that, because God has paid the debts of sin through our redeemer Christ, we owe to God a duty of praise and honour. Like so many things in our homes, bills have a mundane (worldly) purpose or function, but they can also be a spiritual reminder of our status under God and our higher calling as a disciple of Christ.

Whatever dilemmas, decisions, conundrums and confusions come our way, we need to do what is necessary in our day and age. We pay our bills, fill in forms, renew licences and keep the law of the land. But through it all, we must not neglect to render to God what is God's, giving God the praise and honour due to his name. Money is what it is, and we have as much of it as we have. Taxes are as certain as death, as Benjamin Franklin might have put it, so we accept the price we pay on earth and pay our dues as best we can. Yet on the other side of the coin is the sure and certain fact, and the sure and certain hope, that *God* is God, and God is *God*: our maker, our debt-payer and the eternal presence in our lives.

Creator God, by your Spirit, help us always to remember that you, and no other, are God, to promote peace and to live as those whose debts have been paid in Jesus Christ our Lord. Amen

Holy Tuesday

Purse

Money talks

> When Judas, his betrayer, saw that Jesus was condemned, he repented and brought back the thirty pieces of silver to the chief priests and the elders. He said, 'I have sinned by betraying innocent blood.' But they said, 'What is that to us? See to it yourself.' Throwing down the pieces of silver in the temple, he departed; and he went and hanged himself. But the chief priests, taking the pieces of silver, said, 'It is not lawful to put them into the treasury, since they are blood money.' After conferring together, they used them to buy the potter's field as a place to bury foreigners. For this reason that field has been called the Field of Blood to this day.
>
> MATTHEW 27:3–8

Here we have the most famous purse in history. We can assume that the 30 pieces of silver that Judas was paid for betraying Jesus were either given to him in some kind of purse or that he put them into one. He also held the 'common purse', which, according to John, provided him with the means to be dishonest with the disciples' kitty (see John 12:4–6). Other purses we find in the New Testament are those that the disciples are instructed to leave behind when sent on their mission (see Luke 22:35–36).

The coins that Judas was given to put in a purse were shekels from Tyre, which were the only valid currency in the temple in Jerusalem. They were minted between around 126BC and AD57. We come across one of them when Jesus is questioned about the temple tax, and he tells Peter to get one out of a fish's mouth: 'Take the first fish that comes up; and when you open its mouth, you will find a coin; take that and give it to them for you and me' (Matthew 17:27). The tax was evidently half a shekel per man. Judas was paid with the same coinage, collected from faithful Jews, and paid out to secure the capture and death of Christ. The coin itself had on one side the head of Melqart, a god of the Phoenician city of Tyre, and on the other an eagle, with the Greek inscription 'from the holy and inviolable Tyre'. It would have weighed just over 13 grams and was around 24 mm in diameter. It is still possible to see and even purchase examples of these today. Money endures, and the fact that we can buy ancient coins says something about its longevity, even if its value varies.

We have always carried money and, until clothes with pockets were conceived of in the late 16th century, purses were a necessary unisex item. While there are many modern household artefacts that would have astounded the disciples, the purse or wallet has remained largely unchanged. A purse to Judas was pretty much what it is to us today, and vice versa (without the designer labels!).

The first 'money' seems to have originated around 2000BC, when in ancient Mesopotamia and then in ancient Egypt it was associated with grain stored in temple granaries. Money was more like a receipt, rather than something to spend, and metal coins were used as tokens to represent the value of goods or commodities invested or banked. The valuable goods themselves did not need to be moved about often, but were represented by coins. However, the value of a circulating coinage could only be as reliable as the storage locations, which themselves might be subject to siege, war or destruction. A coin indicating that one had so many bushels of grain stored was of little value if the grain had been destroyed or stolen! As a result, coins themselves began to gain value in their own right, and it is only more recently that money has returned to the idea that the sum mentioned on a banknote is not actually the money but a promissory reference to it. A cheque carries this idea further. In our modern, technologically assisted age, there are real philosophical questions to be asked about whether money actually exists and whether the 'same' money can be accounted for more than once, such as when banks lend out money they do not really have and so forth. Some financial shenanigans and crises of recent years hinge on the fact that one might not need to have the money in order to spend or lend it.

The spirituality of money is a contentious matter and, if we examine the contents of our purses, we may be inspired to reflect on live issues such as borrowing, lending, debt, poverty, benefit payments, taxation, pensions, investments, interest rates, inflation and charity. All of these issues are to be found lining our purses alongside our coins, notes and plastic cards, even though our individual ability to change the world of money is negligible. So many people are controlled by money, and have little or no control over their finances. With some banks actually charging around 800,000% per annum interest on unarranged overdrafts, and some loan companies up to 5,000% per annum, debt is a huge issue today. I am the chair of a credit union and know that there are many people today for whom a sudden bill of £400 would send them into debt, to add to the vast numbers of people who already are in debt. Money is not so much a possession, or a public good or evil, but it is a language and we know that 'money talks'.

So what does the money in your purse say to you when you peer inside? Does it make you grateful, sad, glad, greedy or compromised? Does its presence in your purse remind you of those whose purses are empty? Are you poor yourself, struggling to make ends meet? Or does your purse, empty or full, remind you of Judas, maligned over his use of money and ultimately destroyed by it? This week, as we approach the betrayal, arrest and crucifixion of Jesus, we might remember that it was his friend Judas' purse that betrayed him. Seduced by the promise of wealth and by the power that handing Jesus to the authorities gave him, Judas 'sold out' his Lord and soon realised that he could no longer live with himself for having done so.

Money problems lead to many suicides today. Our money is not only the currency of life; it is also the currency of death and despair. We can never know Judas' motives, but we can sense the soul-destruction those temple coins caused him. So we should have some compassion, even for Judas, and remember that he did repent but could not undo the damage he had done.

Yet his betrayal of Jesus set in motion the wheels of the climactic days of salvation. Judas himself, like the money he held, is ambiguous and complex, being able to both do harm and enable good. When you look into the dark recesses of your purse, pray for light, and remember Judas and the fate of so many after him who have been betrayed and destroyed by money.

Saviour Christ, who understood the conflictedness of Judas and knows the complexities of modern life, spare and save us from the destructive power of money, that our purses may be always open to the needs and sufferings of others. Amen

Holy Wednesday

Towel

Wrapped in service

During supper Jesus, knowing that the Father had given all things into his hands, and that he had come from God and was going to God, got up from the table, took off his outer robe, and tied a towel around himself. Then he poured water into a basin and began to wash the disciples' feet and to wipe them with the towel that was tied around him. He came to Simon Peter, who said to him, 'Lord, are you going to wash my feet?' Jesus answered, 'You do not know now what I am doing, but later you will understand.' Peter said to him, 'You will never wash my feet.' Jesus answered, 'Unless I wash you, you have no share with me.' Simon Peter said to him, 'Lord, not my feet only but also my hands and my head!' Jesus said to him, 'One who has bathed does not need to wash, except for the feet, but is entirely clean. And you are clean, though not all of you.' For he knew who was to betray him; for this reason he said, 'Not all of you are clean.'

After he had washed their feet, had put on his robe, and had returned to the table, he said to them, 'Do you know what I have done to you? You call me Teacher and Lord – and you are right, for that is what I am. So if I, your Lord and Teacher, have washed your feet, you also ought to wash one another's feet. For I have set you an example, that you also should do as I have done to you.'

JOHN 13:2–15

We have towels in the bathroom, kitchen and toilet. Wherever there is running water, we have towels to wipe and dry our hands. Paper towels, linen towels, tea towels, snuggly soft bath towels – they all have the same purpose, and we never give them a second thought, because they are ubiquitous, ever present in our homes. If for any reason they were absent, we would notice very quickly.

In the same way, in today's passage, the towel is very much present, but it is the last thing we notice, if at all. Like the tea towel in the kitchen, we take it for granted and focus on other things. Yet without that towel that Jesus put on to dry the disciples' feet after washing them, the story would be very different. In reading and hearing the profound account of how Jesus invites his friends (who are effectively his family) to supper and how he washes their feet, teaches them and institutes the Lord's Supper – the Communion, Eucharist or Mass – in all this, the humble towel is barely an accessory.

There are other towels associated with Jesus that are less humble. The most famous is probably the Mandylion of Edessa, allegedly created after King Agbar of Edessa (now Urfa in Turkey) sent a painter to the Holy Land to make a portrait of Jesus. He was unable to do it because of the dazzling light emanating from Jesus' face, but the legend says that Jesus wiped his face on a towel after washing and his image became indelibly printed on it. Not surprisingly, various healing properties were later attributed to the Mandylion, which is still housed in the Matilda Chapel in the Vatican. In Spain, the Sudarium of Oviedo, another linen face cloth, is claimed to have been used to cover Jesus' face at his burial (see John 20:6–7), although it does not have an image of a face on it. Some people have connected this cloth to the even more famous Shroud of Turin, which for centuries has sparked controversial theories about whether it could possibly be the linen grave-cloth in which Jesus' body was wrapped.

Another famous story concerns St Veronica, who is supposed to have wiped Jesus' face with a cloth as he passed along the Via Dolorosa, perspiring from the burden of carrying the cross. This act of compassion, however, appears to be legend. The Bible says nothing about a woman or anyone else having a towel handy as

Jesus struggled along the Way of the Cross, and her name, Veronica, also indicates that she did not exist. While it is thought to mean 'true image' – a hybrid of Latin (*vera*) and Greek (*eikon*) – the name is in fact a variant of Berenice, a wholly Greek name from *pherein* ('bring') and *nike* ('victory'). 'Bringer of victory' is a name we would be more likely to apply to Christ himself, for in taking up his cross, dying upon it and rising on the third day, it is he who deserves such a moniker.

The victory that Christ brings is not a warlike, triumphant one, but rather is found in servanthood. The towel that he put on in that upper room is much more important than linen cloths of dubious provenance that have become objects of devotion. It was a humble towel for a humble act of simple, authentic service to his friends.

When we understand this, it becomes clear what a topsy-turvy, first-shall-be-last thing it was that Jesus did. Hailed only a few days earlier as king of the Jews, he treats his friends as royal guests, crawling on the ground before them to rinse dust and dirt off their feet, and then drying them with a linen towel with which he has girded himself for the long haul of 24 soles. Peter famously resists, until Jesus insists. Jesus' serving of Peter and the others is a manner of calling: just as minutes later he would say, 'Do this in remembrance of me' (Luke 22:19) in breaking bread, so he does for them what they are being called to do for others. Jesus has spent a lot of time teaching the disciples, but that night, at the last supper, it is more about 'do as I do'.

While the towel gets forgotten amid all the other dimensions of the story of the last supper, it is just as important, because it is wrapped around the man who is king, serving those whom he is calling into service. It is through service that Christ brings the victory, that he truly is the Veronica, the one who humbled himself in service, first with a towel and then on a cross.

Lord, as you took up the towel of service in the upper room, wrap us in your mercy that we too may be ready to serve you in every way. Amen

Maundy Thursday

Alarm clock

New every morning

> Simon Peter said to him, 'Lord, where are you going?' Jesus answered, 'Where I am going, you cannot follow me now; but you will follow afterward.' Peter said to him, 'Lord, why can I not follow you now? I will lay down my life for you.' Jesus answered, 'Will you lay down your life for me? Very truly, I tell you, before the cock crows, you will have denied me three times...'
>
> Simon Peter was standing and warming himself. They asked him, 'You are not also one of his disciples, are you?' He denied it and said, 'I am not.' One of the slaves of the high priest, a relative of the man whose ear Peter had cut off, asked, 'Did I not see you in the garden with him?' Again Peter denied it, and at that moment the cock crowed.
>
> JOHN 13:36–38; 18:25–27

On the top of many churches and some other tall buildings, there is a weather vane. Blown by the wind, it is a simple and accurate tool for determining wind direction. The first known one was in Athens, depicting the Greek god Triton, made by the astronomer Andronicus in 48BC. The Romans soon adopted this practical and ornamental idea, and they made weather vanes in honour of their gods. The gospel writers might have known of these, but they were by no means Christian or even Jewish. It was Pope Nicholas (800–867) who decreed that a cockerel vane should be put on every church tower, spire or steeple. He echoed Pope Gregory I, who two centuries earlier had said that the cockerel was the most suitable emblem of Christianity because it is the emblem of Peter, to whom Christ gave the care of the early church (see 'Keys', p. 28). A deeper significance lies in why the cockerel would be the symbol of Peter, who is more often associated with crossed keys: it reminds us of Peter's human frailty and flawed nature. We are like that too, and the weathercock gives both an historical reminder and a call – a reminder that Peter denied Christ before the cock crowed and the call of the witness (or martyr) not to deny Christ.

Peter was simply the first person to deny Christ, and he will not be the last. While we try to remember all those who in the steps of Peter have suffered and died for their faith in the Lord Jesus, there are countless more who denied the faith, disowned Jesus and caved in under pressure. The shadow side of persecution, under which some become heroes, is that many more cannot endure, and reluctantly let go of that which got them into trouble in the first place, that which offends their persecutors or simply that which, because they believe it, brings pain, humiliation and sometimes even torture and death to their families and friends.

This is the cruellest and lowest form of torture, to perpetrate violence not so much against the one persecuted for their faith or beliefs, but against their family members. Long before Macbeth had Macduff's family murdered in his absence (*Macbeth*, IV.iii), the unjust were inflicting grief as well as physical pain on their victims. Depraved humanity has known for a long time that the best way to hurt someone is to hurt someone they love rather than threaten them directly. Countless millions have endured that and surrendered their faith or integrity to save their loved ones. We should be cautious in judging them. This affects Peter too, because he may well have felt that some of his actions led to Jesus' death and that, while he deserved punishment for his sins (as we all do), Jesus did not. So the challenge not to deny Christ is, in some contexts and situations, unbearably hard.

A weathercock sits on the top of every church spire to remind us not to deny Christ, but while the crow of the cockerel made Peter recall Jesus' prediction of his denial, this is not of course the typical function of a cock's crow. A cockerel serves as an alarm clock; it is a messenger of dawn, of the breaking of a new day. On that particular day, the cock's crow is the harbinger of the darkest day ever. Peter has been waiting in the courtyard all night since Jesus' arrest, to see what would happen, and what happens is not what he expects: the cock crows with its customary 'Get up! Day is dawning!' cry, but to Peter this is a sound of deep despair, because it calls him into a new dawn in which he is harshly reminded that he is a denier, the first ever, of Christ.

If we dread the sound of our alarm clock each day, and think it is a mournful, annoying call into the world, then Peter's wake-up call on Good Friday morning was a raucous squawk from the depths of hell. And it wracked him. He bore the shame and burden of it not only as he witnessed Jesus' crucifixion a few hours later, but to his own martyr's grave in Rome. The gospel of Mark says, 'Then Peter remembered that Jesus had said to him, "Before the cock crows twice, you will deny me three times." And he broke down and wept' (Mark 14:72).

Peter's weakness, referred to so often, and confidently frowned on by Christians and others since, can remind us of some home truths each morning when our alarm clocks hail and haul us into a new day. In the light of a new day, some of what happened in the previous one looks or feels different, and we can wake with a great sense of regret for something we got or did wrong yesterday. Or the alarm clock beckons us to excitement, opportunity and joy: what shall I do today? As you fumble for the switch, looking at the alarm clock through one eye, wonder how you, like Mary, can magnify the Lord today (Luke 1:46).

What is it, in faith, that your alarm clock says to you (apart from 'Get up!') each morning? To what do you wake each new day, and to what calling? Whatever it is, give thanks for it. The hymn by John Keble (1792–1866) begins, 'New every morning is the love, our waking and uprising prove, through sleep and darkness safely brought, restored to life and power and thought.' That is true, and was true, even for Peter on the day that the friend he denied would be crucified. Even then there was new love, greater love than had ever before been shown, as the cock crowed, heralding a day of both suffering and salvation, the combination of which made for a truly 'good' Friday, on which everything would change. May the alarm clock by the bed always be a reminder that God's love comes every morning afresh, calling us to new tasks, new joys and new hope.

Lord Jesus, your love is new every morning, and gives us mercy and hope each day. As we wake from sleep, call us into the new dawn of salvation's day, and give us grace and courage to own our faith and proclaim your glory. Amen

Good Friday

Crucifix

Badge of love

For Christ did not send me to baptise but to proclaim the gospel, and not with eloquent wisdom, so that the cross of Christ might not be emptied of its power.

For the message about the cross is foolishness to those who are perishing, but to us who are being saved it is the power of God. For it is written,

'I will destroy the wisdom of the wise,
and the discernment of the discerning I will thwart.'

Where is the one who is wise? Where is the scribe? Where is the debater of this age? Has not God made foolish the wisdom of the world? For since, in the wisdom of God, the world did not know God through wisdom, God decided, through the foolishness of our proclamation, to save those who believe. For Jews demand signs and Greeks desire wisdom, but we proclaim Christ crucified, a stumbling-block to Jews and foolishness to Gentiles, but to those who are the called, both Jews and Greeks, Christ the power of God and the wisdom of God. For God's foolishness is wiser than human wisdom, and God's weakness is stronger than human strength.

1 CORINTHIANS 1:17–25

Many people have crucifixes, in the bedroom, in the hallway, any-where really. Some schools have them in every classroom, and many people wear one around their neck. The cross has become a kind of Christian badge: a symbol of faith, to remind ourselves of our crucified Lord, and perhaps to show others that it is he whom we follow. Some people wear a cross in the same way they wear a lapel badge of some organisation or club they belong to or as they might wear a poppy or other charity-supporter's badge. Others wear a cross, sometimes hidden, because being a Christian is something so inherent to their being that the wearing of it is fundamental to their identity.

Recent controversial legal cases that have presumed to prescribe whether employees of airlines and hospitals may wear a cross have caused great concern, as for some the right to wear a cross is the same as the right to be a Christian in the first place. In a 'Christian country', such as the UK, it is worrying indeed that the cross is sometimes seen as a symbol of faith that might cause offence and that a citizen may in some circumstances be banned from wearing, either visibly or at all. It is a basic human right to have freedom of thought, conscience and religion, but there are those who would draw a distinction between what one believes inside and what one wears on the outside. Nevertheless, in 2005 a school in Derby suspended a student when she refused to remove a cross she was wearing. Three years later, a court in Spain ruled that crosses should be removed from state schools.

On the other hand, in the Canadian province of Quebec in 2008, a judgement declared that it was not a breach of others' human rights to have crucifixes in public places, such as schools, law courts and parliament buildings. Likewise, in an Italian case in 2011, the European Court of Human Rights ruled that crucifixes are acceptable in state classrooms, describing them as an 'essentially passive symbol' with no obvious religious influence. Still, in 2013, airline employee Nadia Eweida had to go to the same court to maintain the right to wear a cross at work, and obtained a ruling that to manifest one's religion is a 'fundamental right'. After nearly 2,000 years, the cross of Christ is still controversial.

However, as we are all too vividly reminded on this most holy of days, the cross is not simply a symbol or a badge of faith. The cross has been domesticated so much that it is worn as jewellery or hung on a wall. While crucifixes were originally made as objects to aid devotion and assist prayer, over time some have been made and used as ornaments, objects of aesthetic beauty or furnishings. Some crosses – in our homes, for example – are so much part of the furniture that they go unnoticed. As such, as the apostle Paul might put it, the cross is emptied of its power.

In this, the fate of the cross in modern society mirrors the attitudes shown towards it in its own day. It is an embarrassment, emptied of its power and meaning. The cross is not a symbol, an ornament or a piece of jewellery. It was a brutal, oft-used, do-it-yourself improvised structure of torture and execution. In Roman Palestine around the time of Jesus, using trees and cross-beams roughly hewn, criminals were unceremoniously nailed or tied to them in excruciating, breath-depriving, blood-draining, heat-scorching ways, and were left in sun-baked public places to choke and bleed to death. While it was the Emperor Constantine who in 312 first decided that the cross was a symbol under which to fight in battle, thus turning the cross into a badge, any recognition of what a cross was for, and what it did to its victims, makes the idea that it is simply a religious symbol laughable.

The cross is as offensive now as it was at the time of the first Christians. To Jews, the fact that Jesus was crucified made him cursed (see Deuteronomy 21:22–23), while to Greeks (non-Jews, or Gentiles) the idea that someone who is God would allow himself to be crucified is utter nonsense. Gods are powerful, almost magical, beings to be worshipped, feared and adored, so a god who is so weak as to be humiliated by being killed in such a mystifyingly horrible way is so fanciful as to be beyond credibility.

After the resurrection, the first disciples had this double barrier to overcome in persuading anyone who would listen that Jesus, who the Jews called a blasphemer and who the Romans called a rebellious troublemaker, was the Messiah, the Son of God. It is remarkable that any of them got anywhere. But they did, in spite of early obstacles and much martyrdom, get everywhere, such that now the story is so ingrained in western culture that the cross has been emptied of its power, as so many people nowadays have no idea what it truly represents. While a court can rule that it is a passive symbol – a harmless badge – we remember that countless martyrs have died for the truth it points to, and are dying still. There is a great irony in the fact that the depiction of an instrument of torture and death can even today provoke both indifference and murderous hate on the same planet at the same time.

Yet, if the cross is a symbol of anything, it is not indifference or hate, nor even suffering or glory. It is, in fact, obviously, a symbol of love. If you have one around your neck or on your wall, you are wearing or displaying an object that declares that God loves you and that you love God. Whether your cross is a crucifix with the outstretched embrace of Jesus on it, or a cross as empty as the tomb on the third day, it is pointing not only to the death of Jesus but also to his resurrection. In that death and resurrection we see and receive a love so amazing, so divine, it demands our soul, our life, our all.

Jesus, by your cross and resurrection you have redeemed the world. As you embraced us on the cross, may we so embrace all who suffer or are in need of grace. Amen

Holy Saturday

Bed

Rising from sleep

> The next day, that is, after the day of Preparation, the chief
> priests and the Pharisees gathered before Pilate and said,
> 'Sir, we remember what that impostor said while he was still
> alive, "After three days I will rise again." Therefore command
> that the tomb be made secure until the third day; otherwise
> his disciples may go and steal him away, and tell the people,
> "He has been raised from the dead," and the last deception
> would be worse than the first.' Pilate said to them, 'You have
> a guard of soldiers; go, make it as secure as you can.' So they
> went with the guard and made the tomb secure by sealing
> the stone.
>
> MATTHEW 27:62–66

Most of us slept in a bed last night, even though the idea of sleeping
on or in a bed is, historically, a relatively recent phenomenon.
Of course, sleeping itself is not; rather, it is a vital and necessary
dimension of human well-being. There are different levels of sleep –
deep sleep, wakeful sleep, rapid-eye-movement sleep – and during
the various phases of a sleep cycle, we experience each of these
several times. While we are asleep, we rest, we heal, we store our
memories, we dream. Our heartbeats drop to their lowest rate and
our consciousness shuts down. It is a kind of nightly pseudo-death,
and the bed we lie in is like a temporary grave.

We must sleep. After only a few days, nothing can keep us awake,
and when we are deprived of sleep we become confused, forgetful
and can hallucinate. No one has gone for more than eleven days

without sleep, according to the *Guinness Book of Records*. Sleep is a human need and, while the basic human right to sleep has never been insisted upon, to deprive someone of sleep is a cruel form of torture. Insomniacs, like King Nebuchadnezzar (Daniel 2:1), suffer terribly.

Each of us needs a different amount of sleep, depending on our age, metabolism and lifestyle. In the UK, the average national bedtime is 11.45 pm, and the average time spent in bed is seven-and-a-half hours. Allowing for time to actually fall asleep (15 minutes is normal) and wakefulness in the morning, this means that the oft-quoted norm of seven hours of sleep is borne out by the evidence. In contrast, the Saudis spend on average only five-and-a-half hours in bed, while the Norwegians sleep the longest, at an average of seven hours 39 minutes. We thus spend a significant proportion of each day asleep and, if you were to live to 93 years of age, you will have spent just over a quarter of a million hours asleep. People who sleep a lot less than seven hours each day are at higher risk of illnesses such as heart disease, and have been shown to have shorter lifespans. Our sleep is affected by the weather, air pressure, the phases of the moon, stress, our diet and how much exercise we have done.

Our ancestors slept on the floor, with animal furs, straw or hair for comfort, and each other for warmth. During Jesus' time, the idea of a bed would have been quite strange, and the closest thing they would have known to a modern bed would have been the kind of thing found in a tomb: a raised stone surface hewn into the wall of rock, what we envisage the body of Jesus was laid on. We may think of it as a kind of bed, although it was more the other way around – any bed that looked like that would have been thought of as being like a grave.

The idea of a bed frame arrived in the Roman empire in the first century AD, so it is possible that Pontius Pilate had a bed not unlike ours today. The Romans combined the ancient Greek style of bed, called a *kline* (from which we get the word 'recline'), with bed sheets and soft fabrics from the Persians. The richer you were, the better bed you had, much like today. But first-century Palestinians slept on mats, often on the roof of the house, and we might remember the story of the paralysed man who is lowered on his bed through the roof into a packed room where Jesus is speaking (Luke 5:17–26). Jesus told his disciples, 'Foxes have holes, and birds of the air have nests; but the Son of Man has nowhere to lay his head' (Luke 9:58). It is ironic that it was probably only after being crucified that Jesus was laid on anything that approximates what we today might call a bed.

When we lie down at night to embrace the oblivion of sound sleep, we might remember that we are going to a temporary grave. Every night, we enter a necessary small death, from which one day we may not wake. To die in one's sleep is something many of us wish for – that, just as we do not notice our going to sleep every night, we may die, as it were, without noticing. This is not a manner of dying that everyone experiences: so often our dying days involve struggle, pain, distress and delay, such that when death comes, it seems like a release into eternal sleep.

Yet death is not eternal sleep. Bodily functions cease – it can take less than a minute for our bodies to shut down irrevocably – and even though some people have fought legal cases and paid a fortune for their bodies to be cryogenically frozen, this is not the way to think of resurrection, revivification or bodily rejuvenation. It is natural to sleep at night, and it is natural to die, but these are not the same thing. Shakespeare's Prospero says that 'our little life is rounded with a sleep' (*The Tempest*, IV.i), and it is true that nowadays many of us are born in a bed and hope to die in a bed.

Death has been conquered by the death and resurrection of Christ. The grave has no victory after the rising of Christ, and the bed of death is a temporary place of short and welcome sleep, from which we look forward to waking in fulfilled resurrection hope. The bed of death is no more a threat to us than the bed of daily sleep. Every night, we go to our temporary graves, dying a little death and waking in the morning refreshed and renewed to enter again into the new life God has given us. Every day and night, we have a foretaste of what is in store for us all when it comes to the greater death and the greater resurrection. Remember that, when you lay down your head tonight and when you arise in the morning, and remember that every day is Easter Day!

O Lord, on Easter Day you emptied the bed of death and walked free in the light of redemption, freedom and hope. As we lie down to sleep tonight, may we wake to the renewing light of the Easter dawn. Amen

Easter Day and every day

Dazzling light

Everyday resurrection

> But on the first day of the week, at early dawn, they came to the tomb, taking the spices that they had prepared. They found the stone rolled away from the tomb, but when they went in, they did not find the body. While they were perplexed about this, suddenly two men in dazzling clothes stood beside them. The women were terrified and bowed their faces to the ground, but the men said to them, 'Why do you look for the living among the dead? He is not here, but has risen. Remember how he told you, while he was still in Galilee, that the Son of Man must be handed over to sinners, and be crucified, and on the third day rise again.' Then they remembered his words, and returning from the tomb, they told all this to the eleven and to all the rest. Now it was Mary Magdalene, Joanna, Mary the mother of James, and the other women with them who told this to the apostles. But these words seemed to them an idle tale, and they did not believe them. But Peter got up and ran to the tomb; stooping and looking in, he saw the linen cloths by themselves; then he went home, amazed at what had happened.
>
> LUKE 24:1–12

Did you sleep well last night? Did you arise with a sense of excitement that today is Easter Day? Lent is over and we have arrived: Christ is risen! Hallelujah!

The past 46 days are now behind us, as the tide goes out on the season of penitence when we have been reflecting on the Rs of

Lent: Realisation; Recognition; Recollection; Regret; Repentance; Resolution; Refreshment; Repair; Restoration; Renewal; Relationship; Re-creation; and arriving now at Resurrection!

At the beginning of Lent, we opened the door and crossed the threshold with ashes and took the call to realise that we are sinners in need of mercy. Then we recognised ourselves in the mirror, found the key to Lent and looked into our safes. We freely donned our hats, packed our bags with clothes from the wardrobe and dressed up as heroes in our Sunday best as we began to recognise our sinfulness. Starting with our shoes, we then regretted the past and remembered that, as the clock ticks away and we synchronise our watches, we are walking into the future. But first we made our ablutions – flushing, flossing and washing – in a daily discipline of prayerful routine, before putting our specs on to correct our spiritual short-sightedness.

Then we were weighed in the balance and, finding ourselves wanting, resolved to try to do better, reminded that we have a sin-cleansing faith that can wash us as clean as the dazzling white garments the angels wore at the resurrection. We recalled that there is always work to do, housework and prayer-work, and reflected on the coldness of death in contrast to the boiling heat of God's love and judgement. Having had our faith shaken a bit by dangerous currents and powers beyond us, we arrived at the refreshment of Mothering Sunday, the midpoint of Lent, and relaxed to enjoy the company of our family and friends.

We pressed on, remembering our loved ones, keeping and throwing away stuff, and took a timely look at our calendars before tuning into the love of Christ, and trying to see the wood for the trees when watching TV. Unable to repair our hard disks, we sought to be wiped clean and restored, and reverted to the more traditional iron pen, with which to write words of faith on our hearts. Then, as Passiontide began, we turned to the Bible, that bestseller, the reading of which renews our relationship with God. We met God the Trinity in the keys of a piano before floundering in the dark, seeking a night light. Opening the curtains, the light of Christ burst in and helped us see how we may be seasoning for the world, knowing that, with Christ as our Lord and guest, every table is his and every chair made for prayer. On Palm Sunday, we contemplated public opinion as Jesus entered Jerusalem, and we thought differently about taxation, bills and money. Drawing closer to the cross, we remembered the humble towel and received a wake-up call to be renewed by the message of hope that dawns as Christ ascends to his cross with a loving embrace. And then, to bed.

Now, on Easter Day, we rise. We rise to find that Lent is over. Whatever we gave up, we can eat, drink, smoke or take up again (must we?). Whatever we have been reading is complete (almost). Whatever we took up, we can lay down (but should we?). Whatever we were like 46 days ago has changed (have we?). The world looks different: events have been and gone, and our surroundings seem to us changed. Even our possessions have taken on new meanings, and we are surrounded by familiar objects that now speak to us, tell us stories and remind us of the renewal we can find on the road to resurrection.

For the Lord is risen indeed! He rises with us each and every day. Just as each night when we go to sleep we die a little death as we turn out the life-light, every morning the light returns and dazzles us with the dawning reality of our own daily resurrection. It is our daily rising that reaffirms our own existence and connects us to the greater light, without which we would be dead. In his talk to the Oxford Socratic Club in 1962, C.S. Lewis said:

> Christian theology can fit in science, art, morality and the sub-Christian religions. The scientific point of view cannot fit in any of these things, not even science itself. I believe in Christianity as I believe that the sun has risen, not only because I see it but because by it I see everything else.

In faith, we see everything by the light of the Easter sunrise. So it is that the light that dazzles us on first acquaintance, the resurrection light that blinded and confused the early disciples and made them fearful, soon made them excited as they realised that this light illuminates everything that they had already seen, and would see in the future. As we rise again, to a normal day that is also the day of resurrection, we may feel it is special because the calendar says it is. But actually, every single day is illuminated by Easter light, and every day is simply just another, normal, regular, recurring day of resurrection. We do not say today, 'Christ has risen.' No, we say, 'Christ is risen.' For Christ is risen every day, from then on and from now on. It has happened before and it will happen again. Every day is Easter Day, and the day of resurrection is every day.

May the resurrection light of Christ illuminate our past and our future, and shine from everything we see and touch, this Easter and hereafter. For you, Lord, are risen. You are risen indeed! Hallelujah! Amen

Discussion questions

There are many questions here, each relating to the daily readings. They may be contemplated personally and privately, or form the backbone of a group discussion. There is no need to try to answer them all, and they can be tackled briefly or at length as you or your group feel best.

Ash Wednesday to Saturday

- What do you think of the idea of seeing household objects as aide-memoires to spiritual reflection and prayer?
- Are you 'at home' to Jesus? Would you let him across your threshold if he knocked on the door?
- Would you be proud or ashamed of your home – the things you value, the possessions you have acquired, the stuff you have?
- Were you 'ashed' on Ash Wednesday? How might or did this affect you? Is it a helpful thing to do?
- Should or could you give up technology for Lent?
- What are you doing about Lent this year?
- Do you seek or avoid temptation? Which is safest and which is best?

Week one

- When you look in a mirror, what do you see? Do you recognise yourself? What do others see? Who or what does God see?
- What are the keys to faith? What could unlock faith, hope and love for you?
- Where is your treasure? Is it locked away or available to share?

- Do you keep the freedoms of faith under your hat? What responsibilities do we have, given the religious freedom that we enjoy?
- Are you revealing light this Lent or are you carrying lots of baggage? Is there anything you can leave behind?
- How much is your wardrobe worth? Have you taken anything to a charity shop recently? Could you?
- How important to you are your best clothes? Do you dream of success or celebrity, or would you dread it?

Week two

- How many pairs of shoes do you have? (Be honest!) What do your shoes say to you about your journey and others' journeys?
- Do you feel that time is a devourer of your life? Is time a friend or fiend? What is God's time?
- Do you wear a watch, and if so, why? Is time a gift or is it a necessary evil to be 'on time'?
- Do you think there should be a reading about the toilet in this book? What do you think about confessing sins in the presence of someone else – are sins too private?
- Do you shower every day? Do you pray every day? Is doing either necessary or helpful? Do we at least owe it to others to do so?
- Is cleanliness next to godliness? Do you like to bathe in faith, or have a quick shower?
- Is your faith or prayer a daily thing, or do you generally save it up for high days and holidays?

Week three

- Do you wear glasses? Does your faith-sight need correcting? If so, how?
- Are you overweight? How does your spiritual and moral life weigh-in?

- Has the washing of your life been made easier by Jesus? What would it be like to live by 'law' rather than 'grace'?
- Can work be a form of prayer? Can prayer be a form of work?
- Would you preserve yourself from death if you could? Has God done this in Christ?
- Do you ever get really angry? What is the best way to manage or cure anger?
- What are you really frightened of? In which modern phenomena do you put your trust?

Week four

- What does 'family' mean to you? Does the notion of family extend beyond the grave?
- Do you have a lot of, even too much, 'stuff'? What really matters to you, and why?
- How much is your life bound by diaries and calendars? How would it be if the opposite were the case?
- Is God watching out for you? Do you hear his voice or do you find it hard to 'tune in'?
- How much TV do you watch? How does it influence your views, your life and your beliefs?
- What would you wipe away from the hard drive of your heart, if you could? Can Christ do this for you?
- What would be your epitaph? Are you looking forward to meeting Jesus or are you scared of that day?

Week five

- How much do you read the Bible? How can you help others discover its oft-hidden treasure?
- Can you hear God as Trinity? What is the music in your home for, and is God present in it?

- Are we living in a world of darkness? How can we be night lights of hope to a darkened world?
- On which side of your curtains do you live? On which side is God?
- Do you use much salt? What is it to *be* salt?
- What does it mean for Christ to be an unseen guest at our table? Is he?
- Do you stand up every hour? What posture should we adopt in the presence of God?

Holy Week and Epilogue

- Who or what forms your opinion? How do you think you would have behaved on Palm Sunday and a few days later?
- What is certain in this life? Are you an either/or or a both/and person?
- What does the money in your purse say to you? Do you control your money or does it control you?
- How would you manage without towels? How would you manage without other people?
- How would you cope with persecution? Could or would you ever deny your faith?
- Do you wear a cross? If so, why? What message does the cross send out today?
- When you get up in the morning, do you feel that every day is Easter Day? Do you think of the fixtures, fittings and objects in your home any differently now?

Transforming
lives and communities

Christian growth and understanding of the Bible

Resourcing individuals, groups and leaders in churches for their own spiritual journey and for their ministry

Church outreach in the local community

Offering two programmes that churches are embracing to great effect as they seek to engage with their local communities and transform lives

Teaching Christianity in primary schools

Working with children and teachers to explore Christianity creatively and confidently

Children's and family ministry

Working with churches and families to explore Christianity creatively and bring the Bible alive

parenting for faith

Visit **brf.org.uk** for more information on BRF's work

brf.org.uk

The Bible Reading Fellowship (BRF) is a Registered Charity (No. 233280)